Dreams. Goals. Life.

Understanding the mentality and approach needed to achieve every goal you set

© **Copyright 2019 - All rights reserved.**

The content contained within this book may not be reproduced, duplicated or transmitted without direct written permission from the author or the publisher.

Under no circumstances will any blame or legal responsibility be held against the publisher, or author, for any damages, reparation, or monetary loss due to the information contained within this book, either directly or indirectly.

Legal Notice:

This book is copyright protected. It is only for personal use. You cannot amend, distribute, sell, use, quote or paraphrase any part, or the content within this book, without the consent of the author or publisher.

Disclaimer Notice:

Please note the information contained within this document is for educational and entertainment purposes only. All effort has been executed to present accurate, up to date, reliable, complete information. No warranties of any kind are declared or implied. Readers acknowledge that the author is not engaging in the rendering of legal, financial, medical or professional advice. The content within this book has been derived from various sources. Please consult a licensed professional before attempting any techniques outlined in this book.

By reading this document, the reader agrees that under no circumstances is the author responsible for any losses, direct or indirect, that are incurred as a result of the use of information contained within this document, including, but not limited to, errors, omissions, or inaccuracies.

Table of Contents

Introduction 1
   It Starts Here 1
      Mental and Physical 2
   Sir Charles and Kanye 3

Chapter 1: Sacrifice Who You Are For What You Will Become 6
   The Comfort Zone 6
      The Comfortable Lie 7
      How to Expand 9
      Feedback 12
   Getting There From Here 14
      The Creative Mechanism 15
      Reality 16
   New Mentality Yields New Results 18
      Habit #1- Focus 19
      Habit #2- Positivity 20
      Habit #3- Constant Learning 21
   Delayed Gratification 23
      The Marshmallow Experiments 23
      Willpower 25
      Motivation 27

Chapter 2: The Bigger the Vision, the Bigger the Success 30
   Your #1 Problem 30
      The 4-Minute Mile 33
      Getting Inside Your Head 34

  Blueprints 36

You Are Engineered for Success 40
  Nature and You...41
  Techniques..45

Big, Hairy, Audacious Goals........................... 49

Chapter 3: Map Out Your Goals *52*

Breaking it Down 53
  Thought Processes..55
  Inversion 57
  Basic Arithmetic 61
  Basic Psychology 63

How SMART Are You? 64
  Specific...65
  Measurable 66
  Achievable..67
  Realistic... 68
  Time-Based 69

Tracking 70
  Use a Tracker 71
  Old-Fashioned Calendar 71
  Weekly and Monthly Meetings 72
  Use a Mastermind Group 73

Chapter 4: The Journey Comes Before the Reward *75*

The Process... 77
  How Creativity Works 78
  How to Use Negative Emotions 80
  Letting Go 82

Do Something 83
  Solution Orientation 84
  Patience...87
  Chaotic Systems... 88

Work Ethic 91
- Massive Action 92
- Schedule Every Minute 96
- Focus 97
- Active Relaxation 98

Chapter 5: Be Resilient 101

How to Keep Going 101
- What's Your Why? 102
- Success and Failure 104
- Baggage 105

Welcome Adversity 107
- Adversity and Fear 109
- The Elements of Success 112

Increasing Resilience 114
- Connect 115
- Stop Identifying 116
- Discover Yourself 117
- Keep Moving 118
- Avoid Detachment 119
- Be Kind to Yourself 119

Conclusion 121

References 125

Introduction

Let's talk about goals. So much has been written about goals that they've become a major source of pain for many people. Everyone has a different method of setting and approaching goals. Some are SMART, some are ART, and yet some more are RTYDGHH. Okay, fine, I made up that one! My point is that goals are something everyone talks and thinks about, but no one seems to be hitting them. After all, if they were, you wouldn't have picked up this book!

Goal setting follows a very simple framework and process. Much like everything else, we've simply complicated what is a very simple matter with all sorts of baggage and hacks. You don't need to overthink your goals, but you do need to learn (or re-learn) how to set them properly.

It Starts Here

So you want to be successful. Big deal. So does everyone else. What is it that ensures one person is successful and another isn't? A lot of mindset books will convince you that deep down the unsuccessful person doesn't really want their success. That they somehow fear it and therefore chase it away. To be honest, this is a bit difficult to comprehend. Who wants to live in a hovel as opposed to a mansion?

The answer ultimately comes down to how goals are set. Goals are motivated by a deep desire within you. The first step is to properly align your goals with your desire. It may sound easy to do, but you'll be surprised at how easy it is to get sidetracked. Our world is full of distractions and all of these claw at us, demanding attention. It is very normal to fall victim to the shiny object syndrome and get sidetracked.

The next step to take is to realize that simple desire is not enough. Goals are dreams with a deadline. The key word here is *deadline*. The deadline is what reminds us there is urgency attached to it and that this is different from our fantasies. The deadline is what makes this very real and palpable. This is what will separate you from the crowd that simply dreams and does nothing else.

Mental and Physical

You've probably played a sport growing up, irrespective of how good or bad you were. If you played it to even the least degree of proficiency, you probably recall your coach telling you that the game is 80% mental and 20% physical. I know mine certainly did. It was all he ever went on about. His advice burrowed its way into my head despite myself.

One of the major differences between those who achieve their goals and those who don't is the mentality with which they approach them. Adopting an attacking mindset when thinking of a goal is what manifests success. This is easier said than done. It requires deep levels of commitment and a level of dedication that is, frankly, beyond a lot of people. The good news is that this attitude can be learned by anyone, anywhere.

This book aims to transform this most crucial aspect of your goal setting process. Your mindset toward your goals is the most vital component if you are to achieve everything you want in your life. By the end of this book, you'll not only have a framework to which you can set goals but also the mindset you need.

This is the missing link in your success plan, and I'm going to give it to you. You might be wondering, of course, who the hell am I?

Sir Charles and Kanye

I'm not going to bore you with all the details of my life, but for the purposes of this book I'd like to begin with the time I used to work as a parking valet at the Four Seasons in Atlanta. For those of you who don't know, the Four Seasons is probably the most expensive chain of luxury hotels around the globe, and the one in Atlanta was no exception.

I saw CEOs, celebrities, athletes, movie stars, musicians, you name it. Even better, I got to drive their cars. I drove the Ferraris, the Panameras, and the R8s. It was a great job at first. After a while, though, I couldn't help but to feel dissatisfied. I mean, these people were super successful at what they did, but they didn't seem too different from me. Some of them even grew up in the same neighborhood as I did. So what was missing in my life?

My moment of clarity eventually arrived when I was headed back home after a terrible day of work. I was tired, lonely, and broke. I had just spent the day driving the cars of people who didn't think twice about spending $300 on a lunch or booking a $10,000 suite for the night on a whim. I wanted to be those people. Why wasn't I?

As I looked around my shitty apartment, I became angry. I was hurting and was furious at the way things were in my life. This could not go on. Something had to change. After all, I've always believed that I deserve to be happy and successful. Everyone does. So what was missing?

That moment felt like rock bottom to me. In reality, it was a moment of clarity. I decided to stop dreaming and start attacking my goals. I decided to learn and investigate. I decided to act and not just dream.

In short, I learned how to properly set goals and achieve them. This is what you will do by the end of this book, and I promise you that your life is going to change astronomically!

Chapter 1: Sacrifice Who You Are For What You Will Become

If there is a truth to life, it is this: to gain something we need to give up something. The universe operates on the rule of give and take, and there's no escaping this. After all, the things that are free often end up costing us a lot more in the long run. This chapter is going to set the foundation for you to understand what it will take for you to hit your goals.

While sacrifice is necessary, realize that you will not view it as a sacrifice if you're doing things correctly. In fact, if you're doing this then you have a misalignment somewhere. I'll also look at why it is necessary to expand your comfort zone and the easiest way to get what you want.

The Comfort Zone

What is the definition of insanity? Well, according to Einstein (allegedly) (Wilczek 2015), it is doing the same thing over and over and expecting different results. Stated in the language of Buddhism, it is akin to planting a peach seed and expecting pineapples. What you are and where you are in life is the result of everything you have thought of and acted upon thus far. You are exactly where you deserve to be.

No matter how unfair you think your life has been, to move forward, you need to come to terms with this fact and let go of resentment (or other emotions) with regard to this. You *deserve* what you've obtained thus far in life. Accept it and move on. To achieve your goals, you need to change fundamental aspects of the person you currently are.

To be more specific, you need to alter the way your brain is wired to think. Your current thought process has created the outcomes you've had in life. It stands to reason that to achieve the results you want—your goals, that is—you need to rewire your brain to think in that fashion.

Sounds easy, doesn't it? There's no twist to this sentence. I'm telling you that it is as easy as it sounds. Yet, people don't follow through. Why is this?

The Comfortable Lie

Our brains are wonderful machines. They can bring into our lives almost anything we dream of. All this power comes at a cost, though. After all, good needs to be balanced with the bad, the positive with the negative, and so on. Our brains are designed to expand and then become comfortable. Once comfortable, all the inherent laziness in them comes forth, and expansion becomes a thing of the past.

Why does this happen? Well, there are biological reasons to it. I'm not going to bore you with science-y stuff here, but take the time to understand what's going on inside your head. Our brains store information in the form of neural networks. The trope of the brain being like a huge filing system is a wrong one. Your brain is more radial than linear by nature when it comes to storage (Murphy 2017).

Any habit is essentially a network of neurons firing together. The more they fire together, the stronger they become and, curiously, the more likely they are to fire. This is why it becomes so easy to think in a particular pattern once you learn it. This is captured by the popular saying, "To a man with a hammer, everything looks like a nail" (Murphy 2017).

This is why the brain stops expanding, as the dominant neural networks prevent it from doing so and instead keeps asserting itself. The key to stopping this from happening is to first bring awareness to the situation. The process of awareness takes advantage of the way our brains are built by stepping aside and simply observing, therefore shortening the circuit of the dominant neural network.

Next, you need to start installing new neural networks to replace the old ones. Right now, there's a dominant neural network in your brain that is telling you to stay comfortable and to avoid the discomfort that learning something new brings. This is why you read books and attend seminars over and over. It's not the books' fault that nothing works for you...you're just not aware enough!

Expanding your comfort zone is a good thing, and is the better habit that needs to be installed. Think of it this way. Compare a high school football player to one in the NFL. The NFL player has more skills and is mentally a lot stronger. He worked so much more to hone his game, which is why he's at the top of his profession. In other words, the NFL player simply has a larger area of expertise and his comfort zone is a lot wider because of it. He has dealt with more adversity and is far more used to having obstacles thrown his way. Ironically, facing those obstacles makes him more resilient to handling new ones.

Your brain will do everything in its power to hang onto its comfort zone. You need to remind yourself and then practice the habit of expanding your comfort zone. Here we arrive at another potential pitfall. What is the correct way of expanding your comfort zone? Why do so many people who try to better themselves fail?

How to Expand

Think back to your days in school. You went through various grades where you were given bits and pieces of information, in a gradual manner, and by the time you passed on, your ability to reason, communicate, and think was far higher than when you began school. This is the linear model of learning, and it works very well.

Contrast this with another imaginary scenario. Imagine a fifth grader being taught basic arithmetic and then being taught differential calculus. Then imagine this poor kid being derided for not being smart enough or good enough. The situation is absurd! How could the kid even begin to cope with the workload? Differential calculus is so far outside of her comfort zone that she didn't stand a chance in the first place.

I called the above an imaginary scenario, but it really isn't. People do this sort of thing all the time. They set goals and they envision new lives and immediately try to jump so far ahead that the only outcome they leave themselves is to fall flat on their faces. You cannot write *War and Peace* right after learning your ABCs...that's just idiotic!

You will be tempted to jump the gun and try to take things on which are also far beyond your comfort zone. People do it not because they're stupid but because of the fact that they want to reach their goals right now. This impatience is detrimental to your success, as I'll explain in the final section of this chapter.

For now, though, let's look at how you should go about expanding your comfort zone. Luckily, we already have a model that works for us. The model used in schools works very well, and for a good reason. It forces us to learn things that are just at the edge of our comfort zones. Once we become comfortable with those things, we're then forced to travel to the new edge once more and get comfortable all over again.

A single movement to the edge doesn't bring much growth, but over time, this method compounds massively. I mean, look at yourself. You couldn't read or speak coherently when you started school. Chances are you're much better at it now. This didn't happen by magic. It is the result of a tried and tested process.

Apply this when setting your goals. Do something that feels uncomfortable every day and get used to being uncomfortable. Remember, expanding your comfort zone is how you will rewire your brain and literally change who you are. Your new habits will bring you the results they deserve. This is a basic and natural law of the universe.

Deal with discomfort at a pace you're at ease with, and do not compare yourself to others. The key is to get comfortable and then expand again. Take baby steps at first, and do not be discouraged about the apparent lack of progress. There are things going on in the background you don't know about and they will soon make themselves heard.

You can think of this process like needing to jump into a cold stream. Instead of jumping in at once and shocking yourself, dip your toes in, then your ankles, your shins, your knees, and so on. When you fully immerse yourself, it will still feel unpleasant but you'll stand a better chance of swimming farther than if you simply jumped in.

Keep dipping your toes like this and you'll find that discomfort is actually very comfortable.

Feedback

To expand, it is necessary to learn. Unfortunately, if you're a fully grown adult, you are almost incapable of learning. This goes back to my point earlier about how our brains shut down the learning process because we start to feel comfortable. Once you consciously decide to expand yourself, you will start receiving all sorts of feedback.

This is a stumbling block for most people since they're not used to processing feedback in a healthy manner. Often, people think that taking a single action is enough and that once it's done, the rewards will flow. Well, it doesn't work that way. Remember, this is a *process*. A process only works if you execute all the steps within it, not just one or two!

A healthy relationship with feedback is critical for your success, and thankfully the linear model of learning once again comes to our rescue. When you first began writing, you sucked at it. Did you throw your pencil away and resolve to never write again? Well, even if you did, your teacher must have walked over and firmly placed the pencil back in your hand. Eventually, despite your tantrums, you learned how to write.

You see, the learning process is very similar to how a missile finds its way to a target (Maltz 1974). When the missile is fired at its goal, it receives initial information about where the goal is. If it strays from the path it needs to take, it receives negative feedback and makes corrections. If it is on the correct path, it doesn't receive any feedback.

Imagine if the missile threw a tantrum every time it received negative feedback. You might laugh at the thought of that, but this is exactly what you do. Learning is a process of figuring out what not to do, as opposed to what to do. Therefore, the only feedback you will receive is negative. As Edison said, every time he failed, he simply learned a way of how not to do something (Hendry 2013).

When you feel exhausted or temperamental and it seems like all you are receiving is a critique of your faults, remember this key point: you're learning new things. You will learn how to do something only by learning how not to do it. Keep this in your awareness and remind yourself of it when you get upset.

Getting There From Here

So you've now learned the importance of leaving your comfort zone. You also know how to expand it. When setting goals you will stumble upon a hurdle, which a lot of people fail to deal with correctly. Figuring out where you want to be is the easy bit. What throws people off is figuring out how to get there from where they're at.

I'll save you the suspense. You will never know in advance. Your path will not be clear, and you will have no clue how to achieve what you want. Upon realizing this, a lot of people pack their bags and attend another seminar that will show them the way. Do not do this under any circumstances. Instead, learn the correct way to handle things.

The correct way to handle this situation is to accept that it is okay to not know. This isn't some examination where you need to have all the right answers to score points. Instead, think of it as a treasure hunt. You know roughly where your treasure is and need to figure out how to get there. Luckily, you have the best tool in the universe to help you figure this out.

Your brain.

The Creative Mechanism

There must have been a point in his life when Karl Benz decided to create a mechanized carriage. He probably had no idea how he was going to do that but must have had a rough idea of how it would look. You see, he needed to create something that didn't exist. How did he do this? He thought his way forward.

You face a similar situation. You want to create something in your life that doesn't exist. All you need to do is to prepare your brain and get out of its way. It has all the tools it needs to create the path you need to travel along. Unfortunately, we don't trust our brains as much as we should, and oftentimes choose to follow the herd. The herd tells us that being comfortable is okay and that changing the way of doing things is pointless.

To create something, your brain needs two things. First, it needs a vision of what has to be achieved. Second, it needs to carry out actions in accordance with what needs to be achieved, incorporating feedback along the way as it gropes its way forward, figuring out what to do by learning what not to do.

This is where your imagination and actions come into play. But before we get into all that, it's imperative to know why our brain needs so much preparation. Why is visualization so powerful?

Reality

As smart as our brains are, they have a significant weakness. Neural networks are formed and strengthened by emotions, largely speaking. Emotion can be thought of as a turbocharger to learning. The greater the emotion involved when learning or experiencing something, the better you'll remember it.

This is a good thing because it gives us a clear way to learning something. The downside is that our learning or memory can be distorted by emotion. We often blank things out or misremember things that happened a while back thanks to our emotions. In other words, the reality that exists inside our brain can be very different from what actually happened.

What is true reality then? If everyone believes a version that is different from what really happened, isn't the false version true? Don't be alarmed, this isn't turning into a philosophical tract. My point is this: your brain doesn't know the truth. It classifies imaginary stuff and real events as true, depending on the emotion and sensory inputs involved.

This is why imagination is so powerful. If you can conjure images rich in sensory information and full of positive emotion, your brain will accept that these things are true. Once it accepts this, the neural network that corresponds to this belief is strengthened and in turn, it strengthens all supporting networks that reinforce this belief.

Thus, a simple act of visualization, carried out over time, rewires your brain completely and also fortifies the ancillary beliefs and habits that support this vision. In short, if you think of your goal as being real and in your grasp, your brain will automatically figure out what it needs to do to get there.

It might have the wrong information with regard to the actions it needs to take, but this is where negative feedback plays a crucial role. Your brain will be open to rewriting the old networks with new information. All of this starts with the imaginary picture you build in your head.

Creating a powerful mental image is easy once it is done a few times. You will need to do this over and over to get your brain to believe what you create. I mean, your brain might have a weakness but it isn't a fool. Layer your mental imagery with lots of sensory information. The things you see, touch, feel, etc. involve everything. If you've never visualized before, approach this via the bite-sized approach detailed in the previous section.

First focus on the things you see, then layer the things you can taste, hear, and so on. Build it up slowly. When doing so, focus on the emotions you feel. After all, this is your goal, so you should feel great when visualizing this. Your goal can be a physical one, for example, such as a house or some amount of money in your hands.

Interact with these things and notice how good they feel.

Your goal could also be emotional. A feeling of happiness or satisfaction perhaps. In such cases, focus on the feeling and its specifics. There will be physical things that go along with this picture so interact with them as well and keep the feeling in the forefront of your mind.

Simply visualizing your goals and then doing the same old thing throughout the day isn't going to take you where you need to be. No, for this to work you need to *live* your goals. So how do you do this?

New Mentality Yields New Results

Developing a new mindset is not as hard as you think. It requires you to repeatedly execute the habits that reflect the new mindset, and it requires time. At first, you'll make slow progress but, over time, you'll be amazed at how far you've come. So whose habits should you adopt? Well, there's an easy answer.

You adopt the habits of those you wish to emulate. If you want to be successful in life, you need to adopt the habits of those who are successful. Study the way they behave and act. Study the way they think and assume those attitudes yourself. Once you make the changes inside, you'll find that your life outside will follow suit.

I have made it my life's work to study the habits of those who are successful. The following sections discuss these habits in detail.

Habit #1- Focus

What do you think Mark Zuckerberg thinks about most of the time? Do you think he's worried about how his favorite TV show is going to play out? During his playing days, do you think Michael Jordan was worried about the state of political affairs? Or do you think he was focused on improving his game?

These questions answer themselves. All successful people have a common trait in that they have specific sophisticated abilities to focus on the task in front of them. Looking in from the outside it can seem like this is a God-given gift, but the truth is more mundane. They simply have habits that help them focus.

Using Zuckerberg as an example is ironic since he has created perhaps the most useless tool in existence, if you wish to get things done. Despite us knowing what a waste of time Facebook is, we still spend our days browsing through it or, even worse, planning our lives in such a manner so as to impress our "friends" on the platform.

Your time is the only resource you will never get back, so it is essential for you to invest it wisely. The more time you spend on things that give you no return, the less desirable your results will be. Take inventory of how you spend your day. Also, try to analyze how focused you really are when you're doing the things that are necessary for you to move forward.

When watching TV, are you distracted by your phone? When standing in line or on the bus somewhere, are you unable to ignore distractions and feel the need to constantly entertain yourself? Are you incapable of handling boredom? Research shows that the greater your inability to just be bored, the lesser is your capacity for focus (Newport 2016).

When I decided to turn my life around, I tracked how I spent my time throughout the day. I discovered that I was spending close to five hours every day doing nothing of value whatsoever. If you track your time, you will see something similar in your life as well.

Invest your time wisely and fully immerse yourself into whatever task you're doing in the moment. You'll work better and produce more in a shorter amount of time.

Habit #2- Positivity

Have you ever heard a CEO complain about how tough things are for them? How many CEOs do you think actively back down from challenges in their lives? Is it even possible to become the CEO of a large company without facing and overcoming challenges?

Evaluate how you deal with failure in your life. Each and every person in this world has failed at something—from a homeless person on the street to a billionaire. The difference between the two is how they react to failure. While negative and unsuccessful people make excuses and blame others, the successful person takes responsibility.

Taking responsibility and believing in yourself are very powerful actions. Even when the circumstances are genuinely out of your control, assuming responsibility is effective because it convinces you that you control your life. This feeling of control is potent and your actions will have greater meaning behind them.

If you're the only one responsible, why should you waste your time focusing on what others do? Assuming responsibility also helps you focus. You'll automatically focus on yourself and execute more efficiently.

Habit #3- Constant Learning

According to the billionaire owners of Berkshire Hathaway, Warren Buffett and Charlie Munger spend large parts of their days simply reading and thinking (Farnam Street 2019). They preside over an empire that is over $100 billion in size, are two of the richest people in the world (third richest in Buffett's case), are pushing 90 years of age, and still think that they need to read and learn more.

If these men operate in such a fashion, what's your excuse? Learning never stops because the only constant in this world is change. Like the theory of evolution posits, the species that adapt to their environment the best survive over the long term. Those that do not learn and adapt, die out.

An excellent method of encouraging learning is to surround yourself with people who love the same. Our environment exerts a very powerful influence on what we do and how we think. If the closest people to you are negative and unsuccessful, you will mirror them. Surround yourself with likeminded people and your own success will skyrocket.

Do not hesitate to sever contact with those who are negative. Such people are a drain on your energy and will distract you. These days, thanks to the Internet, it is easier than ever to associate with people who have achieved what you want. Listen to them speak, think about what they say, and ask yourself how they would react in a given situation.

These three simple habits are extremely powerful and will change your life from the inside out. After adopting them, you will find that the path you need to take illuminates itself because your brain will learn how to achieve your goals. Make it a point to practice these habits and to nip the manifestation of bad habits in the bud.

It takes twenty-one days for a new habit to be installed (Maltz 1974). Practice these habits constantly, and you'll soon emerge strong and powerful.

Delayed Gratification

Changing yourself is challenging and takes courage. It involves doing a number of small and significant steps over and over again without losing enthusiasm, all while being open to the negative feedback your brain will receive as part of the learning process. It is very important that you stay on the path you set. You must be able to stay strong and push through the resistance. At this point, you might think I'm talking about willpower. Well, I am and I'm not. You see, the way you currently view willpower is all wrong.

People think changing themselves is simply a question of learning the right things and then using their willpower to stick to the path no matter what. These same people eventually crash and burn. So what is the right approach?

The Marshmallow Experiments

In the late '60s and '70s, psychologist Walter Mischel, who was at Stanford at the time, carried out many path-breaking experiments (Mischel 2014). The purpose of one of them was to study the ability of children to exercise delayed gratification. Delayed gratification is simply your ability to deny yourself something you really want to achieve, a larger goal. In other words, your ability to avoid the shiny object syndrome!

The children in the study were presented two treats, usually a marshmallow and an Oreo cookie, and were told that they were free to eat them. However, if they could hang on for fifteen minutes without eating those treats, they would receive another treat. Mischel observed some interesting things in the manner in which the kids ignored temptation.

The real bombshell came many years later. Mischel followed up with the kids in his study, now full-grown adults, and found startling correlations between those kids who resisted the treat and their overall success in life. In short, the kids who resisted the treat in front of them for a greater reward ended up scoring higher on their SATs, went to better schools and colleges, and earned more money at their jobs.

The lesson from this is clear. If you can prioritize your larger goals and use them to motivate you, short-term gratification can easily be overcome. You might need to work on a project that brings you a step closer to your goal, but your friends want to go out and party. What do you do? Well, if you want to be successful, you sit down and work.

Your ability to delay gratification has massive implications for your goals. Practice delayed gratification every day. If you feel the need to do something else in the middle of an important task, delay it by five minutes, then ten, and so on. Expand your ability to focus on the task in front of you and choose to perform the action that is important.

Willpower

To distract yourself from the tempting thing in front of you and to choose the longer-term target, you might be thinking that you need to use your willpower and simply brute-force your way through the task at hand. As I mentioned earlier, this is the wrong way to approach things. Let's dig a little deeper.

A lack of focus on your task at hand has two reasons: One, your task is not in alignment with your goals and two, you might just be tired. The first problem is a big issue so it's worthwhile to break it down a bit. Every goal has certain less-than-attractive tasks that need to be accomplished as a part of it. It is quite natural to look at these sideways and want to get them over with as soon as possible.

The way to approach these tasks is to remind yourself of your goals and why they are important to you. Visualize achieving your goal and let the positivity flow through you. Once this happens, you'll be able to work your way through the boring task at hand. Make sure to reward yourself once you're done. In doing so, a powerful mechanism is developed in your brain. If your reward is attractive enough, you'll actually look forward to these boring tasks.

A bigger problem is if your task is out of alignment with your goal. Why would this be the case? Well, a common reason is the lack of proper definition of the goal in the first place. Perhaps you were too vague when defining it or you didn't focus on what achieving it would feel like. So step back and properly redefine your goals and you'll find yourself avoiding misaligned tasks.

The second cause for the lack of focus, as mentioned earlier, is that you're simply too tired. If this is the case, relax! Do not work in a suboptimal state. An hour's worth of deeply focused work is far better than a distracted five hours' worth. Treat yourself well and be kind to yourself, but don't baby yourself all the time.

Do not ever think you need to be harsh with yourself to achieve goals. Instead, use your emotions from your visualization to power you through. Emotions drive your underlying motivation, which is all you need to stay on course. It's easy to take on more than you can handle so be sure not to spread yourself too thin, and make adjustments when necessary. Now, as you can see...willpower doesn't really come into the scenario!

The truth is that your willpower is meant to be used in short bursts. For example, if you're nearing the end of your task and it's been a long day and you really want to go to sleep, using your willpower to push for a few minutes more will ensure larger rewards. You will complete your task and go to sleep knowing you did your best that day. When used in short bursts like this, your willpower gets stronger and you'll be able to deploy it more efficiently.

Willpower is not meant to be used extensively. If you need to work deeply for a few hours on a task, this is not a situation to exercise your willpower. If you find yourself unable to focus or find yourself feeling pressured and irritable, you are out of alignment and you need to reexamine your motivation and tap into the emotion that drove you to set your goals in the first place.

Motivation is such a tricky thing! Over time, it becomes difficult to sustain so you need to deploy efficient methods of ensuring it remains in place.

Motivation

I still remember the time I walked into a grocery store and saw an old woman, roughly the age of my grandma, bagging groceries. It was obvious she was both tired and in pain. She still had a couple of hours to go until the end of her shift and, despite her pain, she continued to work, complaining the entire time. I remember thinking to myself, surely, she wouldn't be here if she did not have to be. Next, I remember feeling terrified that my mom—or even worse, myself—could end up in a similar position if the right decisions didn't get made. Sometimes realizing the position you *don't* want to be in helps you get to the position that you *do* want to be in.

Motivation is often thought of in positive terms. Using the positive emotion to fuel you does wonders and over time, this is what works. However, no one is perfect. It takes an uncommonly evolved person to remain positive and happy at all times. The truth is that our brains react to negativity in greater force than they do to positivity.

This is a weakness for sure in our evolution, but you can use it to your advantage. When you feel your motivation waning and trying to feel positive is just not doing the trick, ask yourself where you would be if you didn't follow through on your tasks. Where would your family be? Will you be able to look them in the eye and tell them you failed them?

Sometimes, we need to get scared straight. Remember that this sort of negatively inspired motivation is detrimental when used in the long run. Use it in short bursts, like you would your willpower. If you need to use it over and over again, then you need to examine the quality of your goals and the size of your vision.

If your goals don't motivate you, then no amount of scaring yourself is going to get you to work toward them. Always choose massive goals and be ambitious.

This is how you were meant to live and is how you've been engineered on a cellular level.

So get in line with that and dream big. Now, let's take a deeper look at the size of your goals because too many people shortchange themselves in this area.

Chapter 2: The Bigger the Vision, the Bigger the Success

I've written this book because I believe there is a massive problem with goals and the way people go about trying to achieve them. In this chapter, I'm about to touch upon one of the biggest problems there is: the size of the goal. You see, everything that is wrong about the goal setting process emanates from here.

When done right, things like motivation should not be a problem. In fact, they shouldn't even cross your mind as problems. If you struggle with this, then there's a major hole in your thought process with regard to goal setting. So let's begin by looking at what this hole is.

Your #1 Problem

I'll cut to the chase: your goals are simply not big enough. They aren't audacious or daring enough. Instead of aiming for the stars, you're aiming for the moon because you know you've already been there and can see how to get there. This is such a common disease in people, and it fascinates me that no one realizes this.

People have a pathological need to know things. We want to know how things will turn out before they happen. Am I making the right move? How do I know? This need to know is in direct conflict with the way the world really operates. You *never* know. That's the truth. In fact, if you make a big decision on the basis of knowing exactly how things will play out, you're shortchanging yourself.

The solution to all of the problems that arise when it comes to goal setting—such as a lack of motivation, lack of direction, laziness, and so on—is to simply set a huge goal. The more unrealistic the better. You've been setting goals thus far because of your need to be "practical" and "reasonable." What you need to be is obsessed and completely unreasonable.

Your goal needs to be so unreasonable that nothing but obsessive desire is going to result in its achievement. Does this feel uncomfortable? Welcome to the edge of your comfort zone! You spent a good portion of the previous chapter learning about why your comfort zone needs to be expanded. Well, now you know how it feels. People will call you crazy and worse things, but pay no heed to them. This is *your* life, after all!

A big goal removes all of these obstacles precisely because it is so audacious to begin with. When you have something of that size looming on your horizon and you know you need to do a lot of work to get it done, chances are you won't have problems focusing. Another boost to your focus and motivation will be the rewards it offers.

Too many goals have rewards that don't feel good enough. When visualizing your goals, if they don't get you jumping out of your seat for joy or if they don't make you want to dance around your home, then you're doing it wrong. A powerful goal, when visualized, should give rise an almost visceral feeling of happiness, which makes your heart jump for joy. You should feel as if you cannot control the positive emotion within your body.

Now that is a goal worth waking up for in the morning! Do you think a goal that produces such emotion will need willpower to achieve? Well, it might in small doses, but do you really think you'll lack motivation as time goes on? All of the great things that have been produced by human civilization (as well as the most horrible things) have been produced by a daring vision. That just proves how powerful this method is. The key to making it work for you is to believe. As Henry Ford said, whether you believe you can or you can't do something, you're right (Boomer 2014). Belief is a tricky thing. It has the power to take us to unimaginable levels of success as well as stagger us without us even recognizing it.

The strength of your beliefs determine your ability to hit your goals. Now we're going to spend some time dissecting beliefs and looking at their various characteristics.

The 4-Minute Mile

Until 1954, there was a belief that had stood the test of time—that it was physically impossible for a human to run a mile in under four minutes. There was science and research to back this up. The human body was not designed to run at this speed for such a long period of time, and doing so might negatively affect one's health.

One of the biggest justifications for this belief was the phenomenon of lactic acidosis (Whelan 2018). This refers to a biological process where once our muscles stop receiving a supply of oxygen, lactic acid that is produced under stress will literally eat them away. To run a mile in under four minutes would produce exceedingly high levels of lactic acid in the bloodstream, and it was concluded that human beings were simply not engineered to do this, much like how pigs don't fly.

On May 6th, 1954, Roger Bannister, an Olympic athlete (and a neurologist to boot), ran a sub-four-minute mile. Sir Bannister was a remarkable human being so his feat could be chalked up to him being a freak of nature. Well, within a year, another person ran a sub-four-minute mile.

As of this writing, it is common to see high school mile runners achieve this mark, let alone Olympic athletes. What exactly happened here? How could such a strong belief, backed by science and research, be shattered like this? Well, the only thing capable of shattering a strong belief is an even stronger counter-belief. Above all else, Bannister believed he could run a mile in under four minutes.

Being a neurologist probably helped him along the way, but this event illustrates the power of beliefs. A belief is something that can be backed either by proof or lack thereof. What I mean is, we choose to believe things both with and without evidence. The ones that offer us solid support or reasons to believe in them tend to resonate more with us.

Your belief system is what will help you achieve your goals, of this there is no doubt. If the four-minute mile episode proves anything, it is that your beliefs are far more important than any other thing you possess, and that you can create anything you want by believing in it enough and taking action.

Failure to achieve our goals is often a result of a lack of belief, or contradictory beliefs. So at this juncture, the question is: What are your beliefs?

Getting Inside Your Head

What are beliefs? On a biological level, a belief is simply a strong neural network that is extremely active. Strong neural networks tend to involve a lot of supporting networks and are usually impenetrable. They also fire the majority of the time, which aids in their strength.

How are these neural networks formed? Our brain begins forming them during our childhood and, in fact, the majority of our beliefs are already mapped out before the age of five (Hosie 2017). This is why our environments are so important. However, just like how we learned beliefs, we can unlearn them as well. Another important thing to note is that our beliefs, or at least the majority of them, are simply the products of our environment.

Before the age of five, our mind is not conscious enough to make its own decisions. We accept everything that our caregivers tell us and view our environment as being the only way the world really is. Given the state of our helplessness, it is understandable why we behave like this. However, once we attain consciousness, it makes no sense to hang onto these outdated beliefs anymore.

The fact of the matter is that if you haven't seen success in terms of achieving your goals, your beliefs are out of sync with where you want to go. What's more, your beliefs probably make you pick the wrong goals that are completely out of alignment with who you are, and thus convince you that goal setting is a waste of time.

Can you see how insidious this is? Often, you will not even realize what is going on since your beliefs are strong enough to be automatic. They color everything you see and do. The worst part is that you didn't choose these beliefs. Someone else imposed them upon you.

What's the way forward? Well, you need to begin with examining your beliefs about success.

Blueprints

Much like how blueprints provide the framework and pathway for the construction of a building, your belief system determines your life and the results you see in it. If you want to get rich and have a belief that money is bad, well, the belief is going to win out.

Your beliefs also tie together to form a self-image. For practical purposes, you can think of your self-image as being the sum total of your beliefs. If your self-image is defeatist and out of line with what you need to hit your goals, you're going to sabotage yourself. Studies conducted indicate that crime and criminality are often a result of a poor image or one mired in low self-esteem.

The first step to examining your self-image is to become more aware of the thoughts floating around inside your head. What is the quality of your self-talk? If you're like most people who do not succeed in achieving their goals, you are probably way too harsh on yourself. Would you speak to a dear friend or family member in the same manner you talk to yourself? Chances are you wouldn't dream of it!

Success begins with being kind to yourself. Forgive yourself for whatever mistakes you think you've made and treat yourself well. I don't mean to say you should splurge on things you can't afford; that's simply being materialistic. I mean to say that you should be compassionate towards yourself.

People often think it's necessary to be driven to succeed, and that one part of being driven is being harsh on ourselves and our own worst critic. Well, there's a difference between evaluating yourself strictly and simply finding fault, and abusing yourself. Those who fail to hit their goals often do not make a distinction between the two.

Once you've consciously made efforts to improve your self-talk, think back to what your childhood was like. Was your family poor? What did your parents or caregivers say when they spoke of money? If you're like me, you've probably heard that money didn't grow on trees. If you asked for money from your parents, maybe they told you it was scarce and that you shouldn't ask for it. You probably also heard the biggest lie of all: you don't need money to be happy.

Money will not make you happy by itself, but you do need some money to be happy. If you're walking around with such terrible beliefs in your head, can you see why you have not been successful in hitting your goals? Can you see why you have problems with setting them and getting motivated? The problem isn't you, it's with your self-image and lack of awareness.

The worst part is that you're carrying around someone else's ideas in your head. You didn't choose them so why should you honor them? The thought itself is absurd! If you wish to change your self-image, the first step you need to take is to recognize your ability to reject such thoughts. Mind you, this doesn't mean you'll let go of them by simply doing this. It's just the first step.

Recognition and awareness of both the thoughts existing and your ability to reject lays the groundwork for the next step. Before getting there, though, it is important that you develop your awareness in the moment when these thoughts come up. A good way to gain some preliminary awareness is to write down everything you observed during your childhood with regard to success, and especially money.

Money is a very tricky subject for a lot of people and the best way of evaluating your beliefs about it is to simply look at your bank account. Do you have enough according to your subjective measures? If yes, then you probably wouldn't have picked up this book. If not, then you can assume safely that your beliefs are out of whack with your goals.

Write down every statement you heard about money and success. Were you raised to believe that rich people were corrupt? Did you grow up in a place where the corrupt were rewarded? This is not the work of a few minutes. Dive deep and recall as much as possible. Once you've written these statements out, read them back to yourself and note how many are positive and how many are negative. Then you'll have a decent idea of where your beliefs stand.

Next, ask yourself how many of those negative beliefs you voluntarily adopted. The ones you did, why did you do so? What experiences led you to believe in them? Were those experiences valid and universal? Do exceptions to them exist? Evaluate those exceptions. One of the most challenging things a person can do is to question their strongly held beliefs. You will feel a lot of resistance within you when doing this, but keep going. This is where you need to use your willpower.

With the beliefs you didn't voluntarily adopt, can you see how they have negatively impacted your life? Think about how they color your decisions and how your thought process affects your actions and ultimately your results. Can you see how you're acting out someone else's thoughts? These are not yours and not in line with what *you* want, so why on earth are you doing this?

Write new beliefs in place of the old ones. Needless to say, make them positive and uplifting. For example, a belief like "All rich people are corrupt" can be rewritten as "Money exaggerates what is already there. If someone is honest, they become more honest; if someone is corrupt, they become more corrupt." Another good belief to write and believe in is "Money is just a resource that works for me." Place too much importance on money and you'll end up strangling its flow to you.

Once you've written out these beliefs, read through them and feel the positive emotion within you. Make connections between how these beliefs will help you achieve your goals. Visualize yourself achieving them and living these positive beliefs.

After you've done this, it's time for you to install a fundamental belief within yourself about your self-image.

You Are Engineered for Success

All the positive beliefs in the world cannot help you if your underlying belief about yourself is based on failure. If you think of yourself as someone who always screws things up and who doesn't deserve good things, then you're not going to get anywhere with your positive beliefs.

Your self-image is an extremely powerful thing, and to change it you usually need a very good reason. This is true for all people. Repeating lines to yourself about how awesome you are isn't going to do anything for you since your self-image will simply laugh it off as rubbish. If you monitor yourself, you will notice the rejection in your mind.

If you sense rejection of the positive beliefs you wrote down in the previous section, then this is a huge sign that your self-image needs repairing. The good news is that you learned your self-image when you were younger and you can learn a new one now. You just need a different set of lessons, that's it. My lesson to you is very simple: you are engineered for success. This is true because every single living thing on this planet is engineered for it. Without this fundamental fact in place, the world would simply not work.

What's more, this is not spiritual mumbo jumbo. It is a scientific fact.

Nature and You

This fundamental fact was pretty life changing when I learned it, and I'm positive that it will be the same for you. This lesson comes from Dr. Maxwell Maltz and his groundbreaking book *Psycho Cybernetics* (Maltz 1974). Do take the time to read it. Either way, I'm going to summarize below what Dr. Maltz talks about in the book.

Have you ever noticed that animals don't seem to need too much instruction about what they need to do to survive? Sure, young lion cubs need to learn how to hunt but they have the instinct within them already. They know what they need to do to survive, which is to seek food, shelter, and water. The lioness doesn't need to teach them this basic fact.

Similarly, birds don't need to be told when they need to migrate to other regions. They don't even know which direction this other region lies in, but they usually end up finding it. Every species on this planet has survival and adaptation mechanisms to ensure they thrive. No one needs to be taught this…except human beings.

Human beings are unique amongst the creatures on this planet because we have a tool that is both powerful but also harmful if not used properly. I'm referring to our brain. Think of it as you driving a powerful race car. If you know how to handle it, you can drive faster than anyone else on the planet. If you can't handle it, you end up in the wall. Wondering why you aren't successful and seeking methods to achieve it are symptoms of you crashing into the wall.

To live, humans need to do a lot more than just survive. It is in our nature that mere survival is not enough. We need to create, we need to achieve things. Sit around doing nothing for a while and you'll see the truth of this statement. You are happiest when you're doing something that is in line with your purpose.

A bird, in contrast, doesn't have this need. All it needs to live well is to survive and procreate. If nature has given the bird all the tools to live well, then doesn't it stand to reason that it has done the same for you too? Everything you need to be successful is already within you. You just don't know how to handle your tools yet, that's all. Therefore, the negative self-image you have of yourself is completely false.

You have literally been engineered for success in this world. Your brain has the power of creation, after all. Look around you and count the things that have been created by the very same tools you have. The phone in your hand, the screen you're reading this on, was created by the same tool that you have. It was someone's brain that envisioned this and then, through trial and error, figured out what works.

Recognizing negative feedback and the true nature of learning is so important. Figuring out what doesn't work in order to learn what does is how you adapt for success in this world. It is how you use your brain, your most powerful tool. Going back to our race car example, if you veer off the racing line and are headed off the road, you'll pump the brakes and point the car in the right direction.

Similarly, if you receive a poor result in something you did, it's simply a sign that you need to realign yourself. Focusing on the disappointment is missing the point completely. I'm not saying you shouldn't feel bad. Negative emotions are just as valid as positive ones are. Just don't identify with them overtly and dwell on them all the time. Focus on feeling as well as you can (you're not always going to feel great) in the moment, and you'll enable your adaptive ability to thrive and guide you toward where you need to go. Can you see how you're literally built for success? You have the full power of nature behind you. It's just that you're misusing your tools. You're like the novice who is using a hammer to turn a screw and is then complaining that the hammer and screw are faulty.

So how do you allow your adaptive mechanism to flow freely? What exercises and techniques can you use? I'll cover these in the next section, but before we proceed there, I'd like to clarify something.

You would have noticed that I'm not giving you any particular beliefs to adopt. I'm not listing out anything saying this is how you *must* do things. The reason for this is because you already know what is best for you. To be more precise, your brain does. Once you align yourself with your true self-image and understand the connection between how nature has designed other creatures and yourself for success, you will free your mind to bring forth better solutions for your life.

The creative process exists within you and you have the power to build whatever you want. We often cloud this creative process by worrying about time. I mean to say that we keep wondering when we're going to get there. Going back to our race car example, do you think a Formula One driver worries about when he's going to get to the finish line, or is he more concerned with driving his machine through a corner when he's in a race?

His overall aim is to win the race and finish as quickly as possible, but once that goal is set, his full focus is on executing a perfect racing line through corners. He's not sitting there worrying about when he'll get to spray the champagne. Your approach must be the same. I'll cover this in more detail in the final chapter, but at this point you must understand the importance of relaxing into your journey. Set the goals you want and then focus fully on executing what's right in front of you.

Techniques

In practicing any technique with regard to your beliefs, your approach needs to have two aims. First, you need to allow your creative and adaptive process to guide you. Second, you need to install good beliefs. Thankfully, the second goal is quite easy to achieve and we've already seen how this works.

Visualization followed by action is the best way to install a new belief. Doing it once or twice is not going to help you; you need to repeat the action over and over again. Remember, it takes 21 days for a new belief to be installed, so you need to perform the new habit for at least this long. A good idea is to set aside time to deliberately practice visualization. Keep building your skill in this area as mentioned previously by layering new information every time you visualize.

The good news is that you're already a master of visualization. When you experience anxious thoughts, what is that but visualization? You feel the emotion strongly and build nightmare scenarios for yourself. Simply do this in a positive manner and you'll see better results.

When visualizing, the trick is to see yourself living the new beliefs. Imagine yourself in a common life situation and assert your new belief into this picture. For example, if you're anxious in group settings, you might have a belief of "Everyone is laughing at me because I'm incapable of doing this." In your mind's eye, see yourself as not only presenting things confidently but also noticing that you are rejecting the negative belief when it pops up.

In other words, see yourself rejecting the negative belief and enforcing the positive belief as you act confidently. Don't focus on just the result but the entire belief chain that leads up to it. Needless to say, feel the positive emotions this brings.

Another good way to install new beliefs is to write them out. I'm talking about pen and paper, not typing. It doesn't matter how crappy your handwriting is. The act of writing literally builds neural networks in our brain (Harris 2018). This is why writing is such a powerful method of learning a piece of information. Remember to write your new beliefs in the present tense. Don't write them in the future or past.

A method of increasing the efficacy of your writing is to feel the positive emotions as you write your new beliefs and goals. Sure, it will take you longer to write stuff out, but it's worth doing so.

Now, let's look at how you can free up your creative mechanism. On the surface of it, this method is very simple but since we're not used to practicing this, it requires conscious work to implement. In a nutshell, you need to relax. *Great*, you might be thinking, *I'll just go to sleep!* Well, sleeping isn't the same as relaxation so additional zz's are not on the menu for you unfortunately.

Relaxing in the present moment is a powerful technique that lets your conscious worries go and your subconscious mind, which is where your adaptive process resides, take over. This is often referred to as a flow state (Harris 2018). The best way to relax is to sit upright on a chair, or on the floor, and to close your eyes. Next, focus on each part of your body and relax it. Notice any tension in your physical body and relax it with calm exhalation.

This sounds very simple to do, but you'll be surprised at how hard it is to carry out. Odds are, the first few times you do this, you'll be tempted to sleep. This is because your brain is so used to being tense while awake that it cannot fathom a state of relaxation without sleep. Fight this urge and do not do this technique before sleeping.

Prescribing such a simple method often sounds ridiculous to a lot of people because of our need to complicate things. In life, the simplest solution is often the one that works best. This is not to say that you should trivialize things. As Einstein said, simplify things but don't oversimplify them (Wilczek 2015).

The reason relaxing your body is powerful is because of the fact that there is a strong connection between mental tension and physical tension. If there is any mental stress present, it manifests somewhere in the body. The connection works both ways and, thus, it is impossible for the mind to be tense if the body is relaxed.

Once your mind is relaxed, it simply gets smarter biologically. When we're tense, it is our less evolved brain that is in charge (Maltz 1974). This part of our brain is automatic and is in charge of our survival. It is not very well suited for our modern world and doesn't have any creative powers of its own. It is, literally, a bird brain.

The more evolved portion of our brain is slower to respond and has immense creative ability. However, due to its slow and more reasoned nature, its position in our consciousness gets usurped by the bird brain and we end up behaving like a squirrel that is being chased by a phantom dog. Relaxing the body sends a signal to the bird brain that there's no need for it to be active since there is no threat present. Once it retreats, the more evolved creative brain can take over and assert itself.

Another great way to emphasize your new beliefs and goals is to ask people to hold you accountable for your new actions. Practice caution here by confiding only in those people who are truly invested in your success. If you feel your current environment is not conducive for your success, chances are that the people you interact with the most will not care for your improvement.

If you do have people that truly support you, then let them know of your goals. Tell them of your progress and give them the freedom to call you out on your BS. All of us tell little lies to ourselves, and having an external reminder of it is an excellent way to keep you on track. If you find your motivation level waning, speak to your support system and assess where it is you're going wrong.

Personally, the method that works for me is to stick a list of my goals on my bathroom mirror and around my workspace. This way, my goals are always in my face, reminding me of the stuff I need to get done. Do whatever is necessary for you to get things done. Remember to visualize and relax, and you'll find yourself well on your way.

Having said all of that, we now have a better view of the entire process of establishing intentional goals and beliefs. You now have a better idea of how you need to set goals. So let's bring it all together and examine how you need to be thinking about your goals and the boxes they need to tick.

Big, Hairy, Audacious Goals

James Collins and Jerry Porras provide us with the perfect template to set great goals in their book *Built to Last* (Collins and Porras 2009). They term ideal goals as being big, hairy, and audacious and coined the term *BHAGs* to identify them. A BHAG solves a lot of problems with the traditional method of goal setting.

Usually when setting goals we simply ask ourselves what we want to see in our lives and then set about writing them out as goals. Well, this process has some pitfalls that you may not know of if you're truly stretching your potential with them. Also, goals are meant to be long term but in this process, short- and long-term goals get mixed up.

This is where the BHAG comes in. First, there's the name which makes it very clear what sort of a goal you need to set. "Get fit" is not a BHAG by any stretch of the imagination. "Make more money to live in a better apartment" isn't one either. These are smaller consequences of long-term mindsets. At its heart, a BHAG is really about getting your mindset right.

Here are the other qualities of a great BHAG:

- Has a ten-year horizon as a minimum
- Exciting and action-oriented
- Can be understood by a five-year-old
- Way outside your comfort zone and scares you

Let's look at these in order. The long-term timeframe of this goal really forces you to think about how you want your life to develop. It removes you from the short-term fluctuations of your life and, thus, puts you in a better frame of mind to design your life. Next, it needs to excite you. This shouldn't be too hard to understand.

Action-oriented refers to the fact that you need to take some action to achieve something. In other words, something needs to be created since it isn't in existence yet. Merely extending your current life situation down the road is not a BHAG. Simplicity is the key to a great BHAG and this is what the next point emphasizes.

With all due respect to five-year-olds, they aren't the sharpest tools in the box when viewed in terms of overall human development. This is not their fault, of course, but if they can understand something, you can rest assured that you can too. Complicated goals will confuse your brain and will draw energy away from doing what you need to do to achieve your goals. So keep it simple.

The last quality is very important. Your BHAG should scare you! The reason you need to have this fear in you is because it's a sign that you care about the goal but are afraid you won't achieve it. I'm not talking about using fear to motivate yourself, but using it as an indicator that you will be expanding your comfort zone by pursuing this goal.

This is what goals are meant to do. They stretch you and expand your consciousness. You might be wondering at this point that if you set your BHAG, how should you navigate the short and medium term?

We'll take a look at this next.

Chapter 3: Map Out Your Goals

Goal setting is a process. Achieving goals is also a process. Like with any process, planning beforehand and preparing is your best bet to succeed. As the popular saying goes, "Failing to plan is planning to fail." To understand how to go about achieving your goals, we need to first begin with the BHAG and then align our shorter-term goals within it.

The thing that confuses people a lot is the fact that goals need to be specific and realistic. Well, the BHAG is not realistic at all. So how does this reconcile with the previous sentence? This is just one of the many things you will learn in this chapter.

Above all else, remember that you need to measure progress. You can only improve what you track. Often, we hesitate from tracking things because we're afraid of what the message will be. The way to overcome this hesitation is to ask yourself what it will cost you to remain ignorant of your progress.

First, let's look at how you need to approach your BHAG and then break it down into smaller pieces.

Breaking it Down

When setting your BHAG, it is crucial that you follow the steps indicated in the previous chapter. Ask yourself whether it satisfies all the points that a BHAG needs to hit. Let me get something out of the way: a BHAG is not realistic. Not in the least. If it were realistic, it would be against the point of setting one in the first place.

The key to setting a great BHAG is to balance the audacity and unrealism within it. For example, if you set an arbitrary goal of having a net worth of $500 billion within twenty years, that is a pretty unrealistic goal and satisfies one point of the BHAG. However, does this really resonate with you? Do you feel scared thinking about this? Probably not.

This goal is so far outside your comfort zone that your brain cannot even comprehend its existence. Therefore, whether you hit it or not is immaterial. You simply won't care about it. This is the reason for requiring the BHAG to scare you. If you were to shrink that net worth number down to say $5 million, does this number scare you? Once it scares you, ask yourself whether it inspires you. The thing to look for is to strike the optimum balance between the scariness, audacity, and inspiration. Getting this balance right is tough. It's very easy to get two out of three in a short while but getting all three right requires that you feel your way through the process.

Monitor yourself when thinking about possible BHAGs, and you'll get it right eventually. A good idea is to go out into nature, some place you won't be disturbed, and think about what you want your life to be like. This won't happen in a few days and, sometimes, you might find that you need to modify your BHAG slightly—even after a few weeks.

Modifying a BHAG slightly is not a big deal. Often, the goal is so far out that your day-to-day activities won't impact it too much by themselves. So don't be worried about not getting it right the first time. When you land upon your ideal BHAG, you will feel a sense of lightness and joy. There will be intimidation as well. Perhaps this is a better word to use than fear.

Intimidation implies you're scared of something due to not having full knowledge of it. Fear might be misconstrued as having sweaty palms and such. Often, when you think along the lines of defining a BHAG, your intuition will speak to you and guide you. Most of us have no idea what our intuition is or what it feels like so this will take some time getting adjusted to.

Do not rush to define your BHAG by making the mistake of thinking that you're losing time. It is better to spend a month or two in conscious thought about your BHAG than to define a wrong one within a few days. The latter scenario will cost you years of your life. Remember, all of this is a process so adopting a "measure twice, cut once" approach is the best way to go about this.

Once your BHAG is defined, it is time to break it down into smaller mile markers and build a full framework.

Thought Processes

A BHAG by definition is ultra-long term, so some of your smaller term goals will still be pretty long term. As you keep breaking down your goals, the level of reality within them needs to increase. For example, your goal for one week needs to be pretty realistic as opposed to your goal for one year. This is where we tend to shoot ourselves in the foot!

You are far better at predicting what is realistic in the short term than in the long term. The reasons for this are pretty obvious. The longer the term, the greater the odds of something unexpected happening and wrecking your plans. My advice is to not bother with being too realistic beyond the quarterly timeframe.

This is simply because beyond that, you don't have any information to work with and you will be assuming a lot of things. So your yearly goals will not be very realistic or fleshed out. This is completely fine. However, your yearly goals should be more realistic than your BHAG. If you work backward from your BHAG, it's easy enough to figure out. My point is that you should not get too caught up with the realness factor of your goals. Know that your goals will be ultra-realistic in the shorter timeframes and aim for realism there.

How should you break up your goals in terms of timeframe? Well, it starts with your BHAG. If your BHAG is at the minimum amount of time it needs—which could be ten years, five years, a yearly goal, quarterly, monthly, weekly, or daily—it isn't necessary to follow this structure exactly, so work with whatever feels right to you. The process that you can track and repeat the easiest is the one you'll stick with.

Let's say you want your net worth to be at the $500 million mark in ten years. Well, an appropriate five-year goal would be to have a net worth of at least $100 million. A realistic yearly goal would be to have a net worth of $20 million. Below this timeframe, we encounter a problem because it is unrealistic to start defining net worth numbers for a week, or even for a month.

This brings up a great point, which is the difference between results and actions. While a lot of our goals focus on the outcomes, at some point it is necessary to switch tracks and think about the actions we need to take. When does this switch occur? Well, it depends on the individual goal at hand. Often, it is best to make the switch as quickly as possible when working backward from the BHAG.

Another approach is to have the BHAG itself contain elements that focus on specific actions that need to be completed, but this is not advisable since this is unlikely to inspire you. For example, a BHAG of "win the gold medal at the 100m finals in the Olympics in ten years" is a better BHAG than "run the 100m in 9.5 seconds in ten years."

Both are action-oriented, but the latter is far more specific. This is not a good thing to do with your longer-term goals for reasons outlined previously. Who knows what a gold medal winning time will be in ten years? If Usain Bolt decides to clone a younger version of himself and doesn't celebrate early, who knows how fast a clone Bolt would run?

My point is, seek emotional resonance with your BHAG and beyond cursory definition—don't seek too much specificity within it. Instead, focus on increasing the specificity within your shorter-term goals as you keep decreasing the timeframe. It is easier to do this if you adopt some simple thinking techniques as listed in the following sections.

Inversion

Inversion is a standard method of solving a problem in algebra and it works wonderfully in other areas as well. The premise of it is simple. To figure something out, first define what it isn't. In the words of Charlie Munger, instead of trying to be smart, be not stupid (Oshin 2019). When you look at your BHAG and try to break it down, instead of trying to figure out what milestones you need to hit along the way, first define what conditions should NOT exist.

Identifying what conditions should not exist reduces the scope of the problem massively and works in line with the learning process (learn what not to do to learn what to do). Let's stick with our $500 million net worth example from the previous section. First of all, what conditions will NOT exist when you reach this goal?

Well, you probably will not have just one source of income since it's going to be pretty tough to get there with just a solitary paycheck. Therefore, you need to have multiple streams of lucrative income. Multiple streams almost certainly implies that you will need to own a business or businesses, even if you decide to hold down an active job. If you are working at a job, given that it is a source of lucrative income, your skills will be at a pretty high level and valuable to your company.

Next, your mindset is not going to be one of poverty and you're not going to be thinking of earning money as being something difficult, or think of money as scarce. In other words, your beliefs are going to be in line with someone who is worth this much money. Your environment will also be in line with what someone at that level has. You will have prosperous friends and a network of people who are wealthy and perform at a high level in their fields, just like you.

There are many other conclusions that can be drawn depending on personal circumstances, but to appeal to the largest number of life situations, let's stick with these two points: income situation and mindset. As you can see from above, simply inverting the problem has given us a string of things that will exist. Depending on your personal preferences, you can break it down even further. For example, if you don't like the idea of having a job or a boss, you can replace the goal of working at a high-level position in a company with owning a business. If you're not business-minded, this means you will need to invest your money well and you will need to become a CEO, at the very least, in a lucrative industry.

So what does this mean for your goals at the five-year mark? Well, as far as your income sources are concerned, you should have established multiple sources by this point. Your savings should be returning a good amount of money, and you should actively be upgrading your skills at work and your skills should be far higher than what they are right now.

How about the one-year mark? By this point, you should aim to have at least one additional source of income and a good amount invested somewhere else. You should understand how money works by this point as well as the basics of allocating capital to get the highest returns.

How about the quarterly or half-yearly mark? You should be educating yourself to understand how capital allocation and money works so at this point you should have read quite a few books and have actively surrounded yourself with content that is geared toward this. Your alternate income source ideally should be up and running at this point, or you should at least have the capital for it.

At the monthly mark, you should have the capital (or at the very least a plan to generate capital) for the alternative source of income. You should have read at least one book on money management by this point and have a fully fleshed-out list. Within a week, you should have a full list ready and have a handle on the capital needed for your alternative source of income. If you don't have a source nailed down, aim to have one in two weeks.

By tomorrow, you should have started researching alternative sources of income and which ones generate the most return and what is needed to implement it (investment, etc.). You should also have joined any forum or identified content creators who can educate you about money and wealth allocation.

So, we've traveled from a ten-year point all the way down to tomorrow. As you can see, the goal for tomorrow is far more specific and action-oriented that the outcome-based goal of the BHAG. How did we get here? Well, it all started by simply asking what will NOT exist. All of this is simply from an income standpoint. I haven't addressed the mental standpoint yet.

Why don't you have a go at it and look at the power of inversion yourself?

Basic Arithmetic

Using math that an average college freshman (or a third grader in China) would know will help you define your goals a lot better. Basic math will help you nail down the realism portion of your shorter-term goals. Let's stick with the same net worth example to see this in action.

In ten years you want to be worth $500 million. If you own a business currently and are fully invested in it, this is a very easy calculation. Assuming an earnings multiplier of 10X (P.E ratio 10), your company needs to be earning at least $50 million at the end of ten years. You will need to reinvest the majority of your earnings back into the business to hit this target. You can break down shorter-term targets appropriately.

In the case of multiple streams of income, this is a bit more difficult to navigate. First, you need to figure out what your income threshold is. In other words, how much money do you need to live the life you want? This is different for everyone as you can imagine. Next, let's assume that you live on 50% of your overall income after taxes. So whatever your threshold is, multiply that by two.

Now, you need to identify a method that is going to bring you the amount of returns that will take you to your goal. The longer you remain invested in this income stream, the better. For example, you could decide to start a new company or decide to invest in the stock market. How much capital do you need to carry both out? What rates of return, over the long term, will you need to target?

Now break this down into shorter-term goals. Will you use leverage? How will you educate yourself? By the end of the year, what will be your income target? How about within six months? What will be the amount of capital you will invest into your income streams?

I understand that for a math section, this is surprisingly light on actual numbers. This is because there are a lot of variables involved for each person. My overall point is that you can work out the math and see if the numbers are realistic in the short term. Then extrapolate this over the long term and remember the power of compounding when it comes to growing your money exponentially.

Basic arithmetic will also give you a handle on how your money needs to be invested and how your cash flow will look. A lot of people have trouble figuring this out as they progress towards a goal. So figure out your thresholds and calculate your way to your goal. Remember that the longer-term numbers will appear unrealistic due to compounding. Don't worry about this. As long as your short-term numbers make sense, it'll work out.

Basic Psychology

This one applies mostly in case you decide to open a company or create a product to build your wealth. To reach the goal of $500 million in net worth, you'll have to create some product of value in a business unless you really upgrade your skills to a very high level. The fact is that it is easier to get wealthy by creating a business than it is by working at a job.

This is not to say that running a business is easy. To run it successfully, you need to be aware of basic psychology that governs the marketing of your product. It is a fact that people succumb to herd mentality. Even the most mentally alert and intelligent of us is vulnerable to peer pressure. Your product will thus need to capture this effect and have social proof.

One way of doing this is to have excellent branding that appeals to the largest number of people. Another is to have a trademark so that no one infringes on your brand's appeal. Making it visually striking always works. Another powerful psychological principle is that of incentives.

If you wish to grow your company, you will need to hire people with the right incentives. Even within your personal life, you will need to align your incentives with the overall goal. If your plan to achieve your goal is bringing you too much stress, you're not going to achieve it since your reward for not achieving it (less stress) is higher than achieving it.

Review your goals and the way they break down by looking at any psychological biases you might be harboring. While incentive bias is the most powerful one, things such as confirmation biases also exist. Using them in the form of a checklist will be immensely helpful. A good way to do this is to question your assumptions and check to see if you're assuming something over the short term that is unrealistic.

A bias is often the cause of this lack of reality, so dig to unearth it. Once you've broken down all of your goals by utilizing some or all of the principles noted thus far, you need to optimize the way they are stated. The best way to do this is to run them through the SMART paradigm.

How SMART Are You?

SMART stands for Specific, Measurable, Attainable, Realistic, and Time-based. When looking at your broken down goals, running them through this framework will help you understand whether or not you're being realistic with the way you're thinking about them. Let's look at each of these one by one to better understand their qualities.

(Please keep in mind, this does not apply to the BHAG. The BHAG is to define your destination. SMART defines your path and the mile markers to that destination.)

Specific

Specific goals have a far greater chance of being met because by being specific, you're giving your brain a definitive target to aim at. Remember how the learning process works? You will receive negative feedback and your brain will accordingly adjust. Well, it is difficult to process feedback if your brain doesn't know what the result ought to be.

Think of it like this: if you're evaluating a student's test paper and don't know what the answers to the questions are, how well do you think you can grade it? Pretty badly, I'd warrant. The same principle applies to nature as well. So be as decisive with the way you define your goals.

Mind you, this is going to be tough the further out your goal is. With the longer-term goals, use your judgment to decide how much specificity you want. With goals up to a year, though, you should be as specific as possible.

A good idea to ensure your goals are specific is to figure out whether they pass the 5W test:

- Who is achieving the goal?

- Why should the goal be achieved?
- What will be achieved?
- Where will it be achieved?
- Which resources or tools are needed to achieve this?

Measurable

The degree to which your goal can be measured also determines its specificity. This is in direct contrast to your BHAG where you can aim for a certain feeling as long as you can identify it. For your shorter goals, though, aim for as measurable an outcome as possible. Again, this is easier for short-term goals than longer ones.

Why do we want our shorter-term goals to be measurable? Well, this goes back to the purpose of the entire framework. Remember that the shorter goals are mile markers as you mark your way toward your BHAG. Therefore, it is in your best interest to know how far you've come and how much more there is to go.

In addition to this, measurable goals lend a degree of objectivity to the whole process. It can be tough to see progress sometimes, but if you have something that clearly shows you exactly where you are, implementing improvement or modifications to your plan becomes easier and improves your decision-making.

Some key questions to ask of your goals is whether they have a measurable quantity attached to them and what metrics you will use to measure progress. Define these and track your progress as you move forward.

Achievable

This and the next quality determine how practical your goal is. The degree of achievability of your goal refers to your own ability to get there. As mentioned earlier, your goals should make you stretch slightly beyond your comfort zone but not too far beyond it.

When plotting longer-term goals, we tend to make bad predictions about what we can or cannot achieve. This is because we underestimate what is actually possible over a long period of time. Having a BHAG is a good reminder of what can be done and gives us a worthwhile destination to shoot for. The way to get there is to hit a bunch of achievable shorter-term goals.

Even with these shorter-term goals, it can be difficult to determine whether they are achievable. After all, how can you predict how the next five years will turn out? A good way to determine this, or at least bring some objectivity to it, is to work from the bottom up.

If your shorter-term goals are sound, then odds are that the longer-term ones will make sense too. All in all, though, don't sweat it if you're unable to determine if the longer-term goals are practical. All goals up to a year can be evaluated easily for practicality. So be rigorous with these goals.

Realistic

Can your goal be hit within the prescribed period of time? Can you achieve it given the resources you have on hand? Resources refer to your own abilities as well. Do you have all the skills needed to achieve this goal? If the answer is yes, then your goal is realistic.

People usually stumble when it comes to designing realistic goals because they place goals that are too far outside their comfort zone to begin with. Thus, they stretch too much and their brain simply snaps back to the status quo because it cannot handle the amount of stress this brings.

If you're finding yourself regularly irritated or just extremely uncomfortable to the extent that you're losing sleep and are dreading waking up in the morning, then your goal is not realistic and you've miscalculated something. You're better served resetting it and starting again.

Be very honest about your own abilities when evaluating practicality. If your skills need a mild upgrade that's fine, but don't bank on a major upgrade to turn an impractical goal into a practical one. Another common pitfall is to use the goal as motivation to upgrade your skills. This is doing things backward. If you need a goal to urgently upgrade your skill set, then you need to reevaluate how you're doing things.

Time-Based

When will you hit your goal? When will you begin your journey toward it? All goals should have a start and end date. Without these, you're shooting arrows in the dark. A definitive end date works in two ways. First, it provides you with insight into how practical the goal is. It also helps establish the goal as specific so there's no open-endedness to it.

Second, it helps infuse a sense of urgency into the process. This urgency can be used as motivation, and it gets you going when you don't feel like it. As much as you'd like to think that the benefits of your goal will motivate you, sometimes it's just really hard to get out of bed in the morning.

If you keep showing up every day and doing the work, knowing all the time that there's a specific deadline attached to the task, you'll ensure that the work gets done. This way, you can save your willpower and deploy it only when it's really needed.

All in all, SMART goals are a wonderful way to get what you want out of life, especially when you combine it with the BHAG framework. You might think there are too many acronyms flying around, and I won't deny this. However, the benefits of this goal setting framework is quite obvious.

Once you've set your goals, the next step is to measure your progress toward them.

Tracking

Whatever it is you track you can improve. This is a common maxim amongst many high-performance professionals and you should operate the same way. The ease with which they can be tracked is what makes SMART goals so powerful. By looking at where you are on your path, you instantly know if you need to change something or keep going. In other words, it makes you very available to receive negative feedback and increases the efficiency with which you move forward.

There are many different ways of tracking your progress, such as apps and spreadsheets. I'm not going to bore you by showing you how to create a spreadsheet for your goals. Instead, I'm going to give you some powerful ways you can use tracking to both let you know where you are in your journey as well as use it for motivational purposes.

Use a Tracker

This is the most obvious one. Use something to track your progress toward your goals. Have them written down somewhere along with all the metrics you will use to measure them. Always keep this information updated. As you progress, you will have to keep designing new short-term goals so ensure your records are updated.

A good idea is to go analog with this and write everything down. This forms a hard commitment in your mind and puts you in the mindset needed to work before you begin.

Old-Fashioned Calendar

This is the method that Jerry Seinfeld used when he was doing his stand-up comic tours while having a full schedule, and starring on *Seinfeld* as well. The method is pretty simple. Take an old calendar and complete your necessary tasks for that day. Once you're done, cross the day off with a big red X.

Commit to stringing together as many Xs as you can, and after a while, looking at all of them will get you motivated since you won't want to break the chain. This is a fantastic way of motivating yourself visually, and it's pretty simple too!

Weekly and Monthly Meetings

I'm not talking about meeting with your friends and family here, I mean to say that you should hold meetings with yourself at the end of the week and month. Make this non-negotiable. Some people even conduct daily review sessions with themselves. This might be a little too much but if it works for you, go for it.

The reason I'm referring to these as meetings instead of review sessions is because we tend to take any event with the word *meeting* in it seriously. Do not ever cancel these meetings, and make your attendance non-negotiable. During these meetings, adopt a question and answer type of interrogation of yourself and be honest with your answers.

Some people tend to be excessively hard on themselves during such times under the guise of trying to be their own worst critic. Remember, treating yourself kindly comes first. There's nothing to be gained by being excessively harsh. If you slipped up somewhere, check to see if it was avoidable.

If it was, is there a pattern you can identify? Correlate this to your other mistakes and see if there's something to be learned there. As an added bonus, make it a point to learn something new during these meetings—some new piece of information or some new way of thinking.

Review your upcoming goals, and figure out if they are still practical.

Use a Mastermind Group

A mastermind group is simply a collection of individuals with similar motivations, all working toward a certain goal. The idea is that the supportive environment makes it easier for everyone to make progress as well as gain inspiration by watching others. Masterminds are used by the most successful people in the world to better themselves. For example, Elon Musk is in a mastermind group with one of Google's founders (Koebler 2019).

Find people who are either at, or close to, your level and network with them. They might be in different fields, but if you share the same passion of improving yourself through your goals with them, it can be very powerful to start a mastermind with them. The ideal size of a mastermind group is around three or four people.

There are a lot of companies that host paid mastermind sessions, but beware of these. What usually happens is that you pay an ungodly sum of money to attend a networking session with two hundred other people. As far as networking goes, it might be worth it but calling it a mastermind is simply a lie.

If you cannot think of anyone you can network to form a mastermind with, conduct a review session monthly with the person you confide your goals to. Have them follow a certain format and report your progress to them. You can even do this weekly if it interests you.

The very thought of having someone holding you accountable will push you to work since you don't want to show up and be the person who didn't do anything or made zero progress. This is not to say that zero progress is bad but if it is the result of slacking off, you will benefit massively from this technique.

All in all, adopting a SMART system within the BHAG will ensure that you are properly aligned with your long-term goals and that you are putting systems in place, which will give you the best feedback as to where you are along your path. It won't be easygoing so if you can use these systems to motivate you as well, then all the better.

Remember that the key is to start with the ridiculously audacious goal. This is what your BHAG is. Set it up wisely for the long term, and you'll find yourself making leaps you would never have thought possible. Along the way, keep learning new ways of thinking so it becomes easier to break down your SMART goals.

Chapter 4: The Journey Comes Before the Reward

Setting goals is actually the easy bit. Now comes the part that is the most mentally taxing thing you will do: you need to go out and achieve them. Don't get me wrong, having a plan is great and as long as you've prepared, developing plans to combat obstacles will not be your issue.

Your biggest hurdle will be getting over yourself. People just cannot help but to impede themselves when it comes to achieving their goals. This happens in large part due to ignorance. In some cases, deeply held negative beliefs stop progress. That's why it is so important to flesh out your belief system before you start to take action. You will be aware of your thought patterns and your actions by doing so.

Achieving your goals is a lot like planting an apple tree. You need to find good seeds and then plant them in fertile soil. You need to water them and nurture them. It doesn't matter how quickly you want the tree to grow, it's going to grow when it is ready. This is how nature works. You continue to nurture your seeds daily until finally, one day, you see a baby tree poking out of the soil. You nurture it some more. It grows into a shrub and then a bigger plant until one fine day, it is a fully matured tree and bears fruit.

It is only at this point that you can eat the apple you've been dreaming about for so long. At that point though, speaking from personal experience, the apples will not be the most important thing in your mind. You'll look at the tree and marvel at your handiwork and dedication.

You need to nurture your goals like you would the tree. You need to protect them and constantly tend to them, more so at first and then less as they mature. Your mindset is the soil they grow in, and to taste their fruit, you need to dedicate the proper time and energy to them. Keep in mind that the quality of fruit produced is dictated by the quality of nurture applied.

Weeds grow whether you want them to or not and require no external attention. Unfortunately, our goals don't operate this way. The tragedy is that some people treat their goals like weeds, sometimes completely out of ignorance. They plant seeds randomly in soil, water them a few times, and expect a fully-grown tree to magically emerge. When it doesn't happen, they stop caring for those seeds and walk away to the next shiny thing that comes along. This way of thinking kills goals before they have a chance to even begin. Accomplishing goals takes consistency and your attitude toward your journey will play a huge role in helping you reach them.

After all, this is where you'll be spending most of your time.

The Process

The fact of the matter is that you'll be spending the largest amount of time in journey-mode. What I mean by this is that you will be traveling toward your destination for the majority of the time. Reaching your goal and experiencing the fruit comprises a very short period of time. It makes logical sense that if you're going to be traveling most of the time, you might as well enjoy your journey.

Those who do not achieve their goals obsess over the destination and constantly wonder when they're going to get there. Think of it as Bart Simpson constantly asking Homer "Are we there yet?" Much like in the cartoon, life will eventually turn around and wring your neck, except there's nothing funny about it.

Focusing on your destination and not on your journey causes a huge amount of resistance to be built up within your mind. This resistance removes you from focusing on what's in front of you and you end up with less than optimal results. Another casualty of this destination-based focus is your creative mechanism.

How Creativity Works

As we've seen in the previous chapters, your creative mechanism is extremely powerful. However, the thing about this mechanism is that it only works in the present moment (Maltz 1974). After all, you can only take action with regard to what is in front of you. You can't act in the future and neither can you change the past. This makes sense logically but our belief systems stop us from recognizing this.

Once you set your goal and start dreaming and obsessing about when you're going to get there, you're trying to act in the future. You're trying to escape your present moment when the irony is that the present moment is what will create your future. The present moment is your chance to work on your goals and take action toward them.

The correct way to think about your goals and the actions you need to take is to visualize your destination a few times, maybe once or twice throughout the day, and then flip back into journey-mode, where all of your focus in on the task at hand or the next task that needs to be completed. This removes your mental blocks and your creative mechanism will shine through.

This often manifests as a flash of intuition. If you've been time traveling between the past and the future, you've probably lost touch with your intuitive feelings.

There is a misperception that our intuition has a voice. It doesn't. That voice is your inner critic speaking out.

Your intuition will communicate to you in the language of feelings. Do not make the mistake of thinking that the only feelings it will communicate to you will be good. I'll talk about this in the next section in greater detail. The intuitive process is not fully understood scientifically as yet, but there's no doubt it exists. What or why it exists is not our concern. As long as it's there, we'll use it.

As you begin to focus more on the task at hand, you'll find that you'll start developing certain flashes of insight with regards to problems in front of you. They won't make sense, but you will feel compelled to carry them out. Intuition is not a huge dose of positivity. The most common feeling is actually slight confusion.

You don't know where this thought is coming from and cannot logically see how it is going to turn out. All you know is that it is there and there's an irresistible urge to do what it says. Even after you've done it, you'll wonder why you just did it but you'll feel a sense of lightness and a feeling of security.

It is a strange voice and once you get better at discerning its qualities, you'll find that such insights produce the best results. As wonderful as this sounds, sometimes, people have barriers that confuse them and leave them wondering about what it is they need to do. Even worse, they mistakenly ignore their intuition and its commands.

How to Use Negative Emotions

If you suffer from anxiety or have a hyperactive brain, it is very tough to tell the difference between the anxious voice and the intuitive voice. This is because intuition isn't a huge dose of positive emotion. It contains a seed of doubt, much like anxiety does. Even worse, when you ignore the voice of intuition repeatedly, it actually manifests as anxiety.

Negative emotions wreak havoc on the mind, but it doesn't mean they're invalid. In fact, negative emotions offer excellent feedback as to what we're doing wrong. When seen this way, negative emotions actually are more valuable to our learning process than positive ones. But don't just go looking around for negative emotions and honing in on them.

There's a difference between receiving negative feedback from our intuition and creating our own demons. The latter is what all of us do all the time. The reason we do is because we place far too much importance on the destination, which manifests as anxiety. We're constantly worried about how our results are going to turn out, and we worry about what we'll do if we don't achieve our goals.

Here's the thing: you've been here before. In fact, you've been in worse situations before when you haven't been able to see a way out, but here you are anyway. Life might not be a bed of roses right now but you're still here, alive and working toward your goals. That by itself means a lot, even if you can't see it right now.

Ignoring your intuition causes it to inject anxiety into you and compels you to do something—anything! Here's where you will spot the first difference between manmade anxiety and intuitive anxiety. With intuitive anxiety, once you carry out the action, you'll feel better. Manmade anxiety, on the other hand, never stops. It is more open-ended than intuitive anxiety, which is tied to an action you need to carry out.

It will be tough at first to distinguish between the two but doing this is a part of your journey. To achieve your goals, you need to learn the language of intuition, and the only way to learn it is to immerse yourself in it. So what I'm telling you is that you need to listen and observe your anxious voice. You need to pay attention to your feelings and insights.

At first, you will act out of anxiety, but once you receive feedback after carrying out the action, you'll be able to learn whether it was anxiety that you created or if it was from your intuition. As you keep exploring, you'll get better at it and ironically, you'll find that your manmade anxiety begins to diminish.

Letting Go

Think back to our example in the previous chapter about the Formula One driver. Do you think he's going to succeed if he's thinking about crossing the finish line all the time? Of course not. He's liable to crash at the first corner he comes up against if he's not fully focused on what's in front of him.

Letting go of your need to obsess about your destination is a key component of achieving your goals. It's not that you should think of your goals as unimportant. However, the idea that you need to obsess over your goals and constantly ruminate over them in order to achieve them is wrong.

Once you let go of your focus on the destination, you'll have greater mental faculties available to focus on what you need to get done. In other words, if you care too much about your goals, you'll end up strangling them! Take a step back from them and let them breathe. Rest assured that by doing this, you're not communicating that they're unimportant to you.

If anything, you're acting right in line with what needs to be done to achieve them. There are many ways to let go of this obsessive need to reach a goal. The best method is to take consistent action.

Do Something

You're not going to be at your best every single moment you'll spend achieving your goals. Life happens and you'll be down some days. This is inevitable. Some days you won't even feel like getting out of bed and will feel sick at the thought of your goals. All of this is part of being human, so don't expect to feel energetic and ridiculously positive all the time.

However, you still need to take action, unless your intuition is telling you not to. A key concept I have learned over the years is that taking action when you're down is what will separate you from the mediocre and the merely good. It doesn't matter whether you finish your task for that day or not. Simply show up and do something. Anything!

Showing up is such a powerful action to perform because it communicates to your mind how important your goals are. Keep doing this, and you'll find that you will produce high quality work even when you're feeling down. Your brain will learn to isolate your task's needs from whatever else is going on outside of it.

A word of caution here: I'm not advocating working when you're bedridden or sick. Remember, there are a lot of actions you can take that don't involve physical work, such as visualization and relaxation techniques. It seems odd to classify relaxation as a work technique but unless your mind is fully relaxed and present, you will not produce good quality work.

A common mistake is to treat deadlines as being more important than the work itself. All of us want to produce the best possible work within the allotted period of time, but at first you will struggle with this. Think of it as asking a high school athlete to play in the NFL immediately. It just won't happen.

So adjust your tasks and deadlines appropriately. If you constantly find yourself running into deadlines, then you're trying to bite off more than you can chew. Approaching the size of the work you're attempting is much the same as expanding your comfort zone. Approach it in bite-sized pieces.

If you overwork yourself, your intuition will tell you to simply stop working on the task for a bit. Do yourself a favor and listen to it. People often think taking a break is being weak and they will try to tough it out. What happens is they cause themselves more distress and end up producing shoddy work that sets them back even further.

Solution Orientation

When you set about taking action to achieve your goals, you're going to encounter a bunch of problems and receive a ton of negative feedback. This is perfectly normal as we've seen, thanks to how the learning process works. The problem is that if our focus is on the destination and not in the present moment, we will begin to expect the problems to simply stop happening.

This is another common mistake that people make. They expect that upon reaching their goal, all of their problems will magically disappear. Well, this is partly true. The ones you're dealing with now will disappear. However, newer, juicier ones will take their place. Again, imagine the problems an NFL player faces compared to a high school footballer. There's just no comparison.

Seeking to make your problems vanish is a huge symptom that you're looking to escape your current situation, as opposed to going on to something else. I get it. You might be in a desperate situation and your life might be a living hell. However, looking to remove your problems will only give them greater prominence in your mind.

You'll communicate to your mind that the problem is your focus, and this puts you in a negative spiral while reducing your chances of solving the issue. The correct way to deal with problems is to do the following:

1. Accept them and then focus on the solutions.
2. Seek and wish for next-level problems.

Acceptance of your problems means coming to terms with the fact that they exist and that you need to find a solution. Acceptance is NOT identifying with them personally or to think your world is coming to an end.

If you are in such a desperate position, then this will be tough to do but, again, do something. Take baby steps toward acceptance and when you can identify with the problems, remind yourself to focus on solutions instead.

Once you focus on solutions, chances are that you'll come up with a few alternatives. At this point, it is important that you take action as soon as possible to implement these. Whether they work or not is beside the point, although it is great when they do!

In order to succeed, you need to keep coming up with solutions all the time. This sounds tough and intimidating, but remember that you already have the tools within you to do this. The creative mechanism, plus the nature in which you have been created, will assist you with this. You just need to give them an opening to work their magic.

Keep searching for solutions and always ponder on them. Think about solutions to your current tasks or problems, and you'll also divert your mind away from focusing on the future and whether or not you'll reach your goal. A really helpful maxim to adopt is the mentality of "move fast, break things." (Newport 2016)

That was Mark Zuckerberg's philosophy when Facebook was still a growing company. In a fast changing area of business where he had no precedents to draw inspiration from, this is what enabled Zuckerberg to build his multi-billion dollar company. He brainstormed solutions, tried them out, accepted feedback, and improved. The key to the entire process is that he sought solutions *constantly*.

The other key to the puzzle is to seek next-level problems. Please note, I'm not saying you should seek *more* problems. Just that you should wish fervently for the problems that someone who's achieved your goals deals with. The problems that a person who's broke deals with are very different from those of a billionaire. You're always going to have problems, so you might as well wish for higher level ones.

Thus, instead of wishing that your current problems go away, wish for them to be replaced with higher level ones. I'm not asking you to visualize having bigger problems, but make this shift in your thoughts when your problems crop up.

Patience

Everything works at its own pace and there's nothing you can do about it. Patience is fast becoming a scarce commodity these days due to the culture of instant gratification we have. When we used to previously wait for two days for our packages to arrive, now next day delivery fails to impress us.

Your goals will take time to come to fruition, and they'll take however long they need to take. You do not control your results fully, and this is why patience is imperative. Like a muscle, patience needs to be developed and you need to consciously work at it. It isn't something that is going to flower overnight.

As much as our society values instant gratification, deep down everyone respects people who display patience. Think of seeing someone in the grocery store checkout line who is constantly complaining about how long it's taking. You'll not hesitate to categorize this person as someone unpleasant.

Yet, when it comes to our goals we adopt the attitude that if it doesn't happen now, it just isn't worth it. The old adage that patience is a virtue is very true. Impatience causes you to act impulsively and destroy your good work. Practicing patience and reminding yourself that all things will happen in good time is a habit you must develop.

Meanwhile, keep taking action and incorporating feedback. Don't take action just for the sake of it, though. Show up and check if there is something to be done. If your intuition tells you to relax or if there is genuinely nothing to do, relax and wait. There's nothing more liberating than this!

Chaotic Systems

If you knew in advance exactly how things are going to play out, what would you do? Well, this is a nonsensical question. Of course, you'd do everything according to the information you received! Well, here's a second question: if you knew nothing in advance, what would you do? Welcome to your next-level problem.

The truth is that the world is a chaotic place. In order for you to achieve your goals, there are a lot of things that need to work in your favor and many things out of your control need to interact with one another to produce your desired results. This seems to be at odds against the thought process of taking responsibility, but there's no clash here.

Taking responsibility for your actions and results forces you to adopt a solution-oriented mindset, even if the exact details of it aren't fully true. It's simply an empowered way to live your life.

What I'm trying to tell you in this section is that irrespective of what your mindset is, the world works in a certain manner. You don't know anything in advance. It is chaotic. So what is the best approach to adopt when confronted with such a system? Your brain is singularly incapable of dealing with chaotic systems. It likes order and predictability. This is why it immediately seeks patterns and wants to know why something is happening. This sort of behavior is simply the other side of the desire to learn constantly.

The best way to deal with a chaotic system is to play the odds. Think of how casinos make money. They don't know the outcome of every hand in advance. So what do they do? They design games that place the long-term odds in their favor. As long as you keep playing, the odds will eventually play out, and the casino will keep your money. They might lose the odd hand in between, but that doesn't matter.

This is a perfect illustration of how to handle a chaotic system. You need to set the odds in your favor and understand that over the long run, they will play out. You might have setbacks and things will not go according to plan here and there but, as long as the odds are in your favor, you will come out ahead.

So how are odds placed in your favor? Well, this is what this book is all about! Having a solution-oriented mindset, showing up repeatedly and taking action, move fast break things, patience, relaxation and awareness, allowing your creative mechanism to come through by focusing on the present moment, always learning and moving forward, wishing for higher level problems, etc.

Play the odds at all times and understand why they work. Will you succeed at everything you do? No, of course not. Even Bill Gates has written shitty lines of code in his life. It hasn't done him much harm, though. Similarly, Warren Buffett has made some terrible investments in his career. He doesn't mind them too much, either.

Keep the big picture in mind, and your problems with focusing too much on your destination or your lack of patience will cease to exist. Requiring that your goals immediately manifest is a sign that you're thinking of them as existing in an ordered or linear system.

The truth is that your goals exist in a chaotic and radial world and the way to succeed is to play the odds. Keep lining up the odds in your favor and over time, you'll get what you deserve.

Work Ethic

The best way of lining up the odds in your favor is to have a great work ethic. It takes work to get ahead and the best way of reaching your goal is to work as hard as possible. This isn't groundbreaking advice, but your understanding of what constitutes as work is probably mistaken.

The truth is that a lot of the "work" we perform these days is shallow work. It involves responding to emails, formatting things, creating PowerPoints, etc. None of this is work that will get you closer to your goal. Sure, if you want to be the world's greatest investment banking analyst monkey, doing these things is going to get you there, but I'm guessing this isn't your goal.

True work requires deep levels of focus that you're probably not used to. In fact, if you work at an average corporate workplace, chances are that no one on your team or organization practices true work. However, to achieve your goals you will need to carry out heaps of true work.

The 10,000-hour rule was made famous by Malcolm Gladwell (Newport 2016). This rule is the result of the finding that it takes roughly that much time for someone to become a master at something. What was left out of that explanation is that it takes 10,000 hours of deeply focused work and deliberate practice to achieve mastery at anything.

Looking at it in these terms makes it pretty intimidating. I mean, 10,000 hours is a lot! However, to look at it in this manner is to focus on the destination. Instead, focus on the journey and work in a concentrated and dedicated manner when carrying out your tasks.

Massive Action

Here's the thing. To achieve massive results, you need to take massive action. You need to be willing to do what others won't so that eventually you can live the life that others can't. This means you need to perform massive amounts of deeply focused work to get to your goals.

The great thing about massive action is that it usually gets you to your goals faster. It's quite obvious, really. The more work you do in the least amount of time gets you to your destination faster. The time it takes to reach your goals is determined by how soon you can incorporate feedback and take action.

Massive action also helps overcome a lot of the problems that beset people who set goals. Usually a lack of motivation sets in after a while and the reason for this is due to the lack of progress toward the goal. By simply doing more in less time, you shorten this period. Think back to the example of the apple tree.

Massive action is like a fast forward button that helps you get through those initially painful stages where the tree struggles to poke out of the ground. By doing this, you preempt any impatience or motivational issues you will encounter along the way. Deciding to take massive action begins with setting worthy goals. Your goals need to inspire you.

This is why the BHAG works wonders. Given its importance to you and your true purpose in life, it motivates you to get there faster and to those intermediate goals faster. Always take massive action and keep incorporating feedback. What exactly is massive action, though? Is it some quantifiable amount of work that you can do?

Well, everyone's massive action limit is different and there isn't a subjective level to it. If you've been busy snoozing your way through life, then taking any action can be construed as massive action. If you've been toiling without reward, assuming your goals are set up correctly, then you need to at least double the amount of work you're doing.

A good approach is to slowly increase the number of things you do every day. Don't try to jump too far outside your comfort zone at the start. I've covered this already, and you should implement the bite-sized approach to this. Soon, you'll find yourself performing more work than you ever thought imaginable.

Taking the right action can also construe massive action. If you've been doing the wrong things thus far, simply performing one right action will put you back on the path to success. So don't make the mistake of thinking of massive action as just being about the quantity. The quality matters as well.

To be honest, I think the term *massive action* is improperly labeled because it causes people to think in quantitative terms. For example, if you need to pitch your idea to someone, you might think that developing your idea, fleshing out your pitch, developing answers to objections, and preparing the final document (if necessary) within a day constitutes massive action.

First of all, imposing a time limit on it is the wrong approach. You need to work on it at a higher level, with greater focus than you currently give to things. Secondly, the time limit imposes a barrier to quality. It is the quality of your pitch that will bring you results, not the fact that you finished it within a day.

This doesn't mean you aim for perfection and take forever. Just use your common sense. Develop it to the best of your ability and do this task at a level that is higher than your current work state. Lastly, preparing the document is an action but it isn't a part of massive action. At best, this is a clerical job. If you have free time, do it. If you don't and can afford to pay someone, pay them. Spend that time doing focused work on something else that is important to achieve your goals.

Massive action is thus about deeply focused work that ultimately determines the quality of your output, which in turn brings you results. It is very important that you understand this concept and learn the difference between clerical or logistical work and true work.

True work goes by another name: deliberate practice. Deliberate practice is the process of identifying the areas where your skills need an upgrade and then practicing them with the aim of seeking feedback. After receiving feedback, you incorporate it and seek to get better. This requires deep focus and it is 10,000 hours of such work that makes you a master.

Think of a violinist who wishes to get better. The time she spends polishing her violin and tuning its strings is not deliberate practice. Playing the violin, especially those pieces she finds challenging, and seeking to get better at them, is deliberate practice.

This sort of work is exhausting, but it is ultimately the most satisfying type of work there is. Let's look at how you can incorporate deliberate practice within the massive action framework in your life.

Schedule Every Minute

This seems like overkill, but it is necessary to begin at this extreme in order for you to arrive at the scheduling level you're comfortable with. Your time is precious since it is the only thing you're never going to get back. So go ahead and break your day into task blocks. A good idea is to schedule runoff blocks in case a particular task takes longer than expected.

As a rule, schedule 90 minutes every day to read and think. You can break this period into whatever proportion suits you, but I recommend spending 45 minutes reading and another 45 minutes thinking. What should you read? Well, anything that strikes your fancy!

Reading is too restrictive a term so perhaps learning is a better word. Watch or listen to content that is related to your goals or something unrelated you are curious about. If you don't feel like consuming anything related to your goals, then read something else that is challenging. My point is that this is not a time for you to relax and unwind. It's time spent actively learning something, whether or not it is related to your goals. If you find *Treasure Island* a challenging read, then read it even though it has nothing to do with your goals.

What should you think about? Chances are you'll have a bunch of ideas floating around in your head. Flesh them out a bit more. You'll find that your mind will bounce around all over the place but keep bringing it back to the topic at hand. It helps to take a walk in nature when doing this and you'll find that this is a form of meditation. I mean, it worked for Charles Darwin, so it's probably going to work for you (Farnam Street 2019).

Sometimes, unexpected things pop up and you are forced to change your schedule. No matter. The point of scheduling your day is not to follow the schedule to the T. It is to give yourself a framework to figure out how much time you have for deep practice and learning (in other words, work that counts toward your goals).

When unexpected events occur, simply reschedule your day. Aim for at least four hours of deeply focused work. What does this mean? Glad you asked!

Focus

Deeply focused work involves you immersing yourself completely into the task at hand and not paying attention to anything else. Switch off your phone and unless you need the Internet for research purposes, disconnect that as well. No one should disturb you, so let everyone know what's going on.

Preparing yourself for this kind of work is tough. It requires you to set things up so all the conditions are met. If you need to use the Internet, you need to guard yourself against clickbait distractions. Mind you, when working like this, I'm not talking about performing clerical tasks. For example, you can work on the specifics of your pitch but don't spend this time creating the document because that's just clerical work.

Instead, think deeply about it and jot down the main points you want the document to mention. Once that's done, schedule time outside of your focused work hours to complete the task. If you finish fleshing things out and have some focused work time left, begin to work on something else that needs focused attention.

Thus, in addition to scheduling your learning hours and focused work hours, you also need to schedule these shallow work hours. These times are reserved for clerical work like sending emails, creating documents, etc. Use your judgement to determine what sort of work goes where. For example, if you need to write an insightful article or paper, even though the task of writing it is clerical, logically you need to think and write at the same time. So don't break this up like you would the task of creating a pitch document.

In addition to scheduling these three blocks (focused work, shallow work, learning) you need to also make time for relaxation.

Active Relaxation

The title *active relaxation* might sound like an oxymoron, but it is the best form of relaxation there is.

Performing deeply focused work is going to tire you out. It is very important that you take your relaxation seriously to give yourself ample time to recover. Remember, you need to carry out a lot of focused work so recovery is important.

Don't make the mistake of thinking relaxation is for cowards and lazy people. People who think like this usually never hit their goals and end up stagnating at their lower level SMART goals. You can include sleep time within this block.

Ideally, schedule relaxation time in between the focused work blocks. What usually works for most people is to have a half hour relaxation period following a two-hour focused work block. Taking this block seriously means you need to have rules for this as well.

Do not think about your tasks or work during this time. If you wish, visualize reaching your destination and your BHAG, but don't make it a rule that you have to do this. The point is to let your brain recover and wander wherever it wants after sitting still for so long. Give it a break and be kind to it.

As you can see, implementing this work ethic requires a lot of discipline so prepare to be uncomfortable in the beginning. Ultimately, discipline is what sets you free. People usually think of discipline as being a cage, but the opposite is true. Instead, think of discipline as a controlled way to plan and do what you want, while staying in alignment with your BHAG. Get disciplined and you'll be able to achieve anything you set your mind to!

Chapter 5: Be Resilient

No matter how much I might go on about how you've been engineered for success or that achieving success is your duty, there will be times when you will feel completely defeated. The path to success is a less traveled one, and there are no shortcuts. A lot of successful people had to go through hell to be where they're at.

There's no guarantee that you'll hit your goals within the timeframe you specify, and neither is there a guarantee that achieving a goal will have all the affects you think it will. Sometimes, you will miscalculate and end up with a result that is opposite the one you intended.

Tough times can wear us down and are a reminder of how difficult it really is to be successful. Throughout all this, though, there is one truth: the only way to fail is to give up.

How to Keep Going

Winston Churchill famously said, "If you're going through hell, keep going." This is easier said than done, but it perfectly illustrates what you need to do to succeed. Another way of thinking of this is that if you've dug yourself into a hole, keep digging until you emerge on the other side.

It doesn't matter how positive or mentally strong you are, everyone is going to be tested along the way. Viewing your problems for what they are is a great way to recognize the reality of the situation and to take a step back from the current situation. So how do you keep moving forward?

Well, it all begins with the intention to keep moving forward. Make up your mind to do so and make it as much a part of your self-image as possible. Think and visualize yourself as someone who keeps on going no matter what. This process alone will give you tons of mental strength and resilience. There are other methods of handling tough times apart from this.

What's Your Why?

Do you know what the toughest question is for people to answer? Simply ask them why they roll out of bed every morning. It is a sad truth that the large majority of people live purposeless and aimless lives in pursuit of things that hold no meaning to them. In order to be successful, using the thought process of inversion, you first need to not do what the majority does.

Connect deeply with your BHAG. Sure, the BHAG is a great outcome, but why is it so important to you? What will it bring into your life? The money might be great, but what will money bring? Why do you want the thing that money brings? And so on. Keep asking why until you arrive at the root of everything.

This root is your purpose. This is what you were meant to do in this world, and this is what you need to connect with. When you know your true purpose in life, there is no stopping you or your upward trajectory. After all, you're simply being who you really are. You're unique and there is no one else who can be like you.

Connecting with your purpose gives you the freedom and confidence to fully express yourself and this feeling of liberation you experience is unlike any other. More than anything else, your purpose will motivate you and carry you through those stretches where it will seem as if nothing is going right.

When visualizing the achievement of your BHAG, incorporate the feeling of achieving your purpose as well within your mind. When carrying out actions as part of a SMART goal, remind yourself of what it is you're trying to achieve from a big picture perspective. In addition, plan out how you will approach bad times before you begin the work of achieving your goals.

Doing this will prepare you for all challenges that come your way. Sure, you might not be able to handle them exactly as envisioned but being prepared will put you in a better frame of mind to tackle these problems.

Success and Failure

Here's something you might not have thought about previously. Do you know that success and failure are simply habits? After all, both results are achieved thanks to you carrying out a series of habits so it follows that these results are habits as well. Once you have the success habit hardwired into your brain, you will automatically do what needs to be done.

The fact that success requires the rewiring of your brain is why achieving success after a long period of failure is tough. Not only are you learning new habits, but you are also unlearning old habits at the same time. All of this takes time and this is why the initial periods are tough. If you fail to deactivate your failure network, then you will likely face obstacles at every step even if you do know what a success habit looks and feels like.

Understanding this process and constantly examining your belief systems will help you deal with turbulent times. One of the things that frustrates us to no end is having something happen but not knowing what caused it. Well, now you know why you will hit turbulent patches in your journey. First off, these periods are negative feedback to inform you that you're doing something wrong and need to get pointed in the right direction again.

Second, the reason you're facing the wrong direction to begin with is due to your belief system. Keep asking why until you arrive at an answer that feels right. Remember that you are engineered for success in this world and if any part of your self-image contradicts this, work to remove that neural pathway from your brain.

Ask yourself if you truly know what it takes to achieve success. Often, we create a lot of problems for ourselves thanks to holding on to unrealistic expectations. If you don't know what it takes to achieve success at something, ideally, you should not have any expectations when finishing a task or performing it. You should be in feedback receiving mode all the time.

However, you are not an automaton and it is easy to slip into an emotional pattern. When this happens to you, check to see what your expectations are and if they're realistic. Often, you'll find that they aren't and by simply hanging on to these erroneous expectations, you're creating a hellish mountain out of a molehill for yourself.

Baggage

The past has a strong hold upon us. You're probably accustomed to reminiscing over the past and running events back in your mind's eye wishing you did this or that differently, or patting yourself on the back for having done something the right way. The past leaves deep emotional scars on us; freeing ourselves from them can be tough.

Often, when we hit a rough patch, these scars rise to the surface and we start deeming ourselves unworthy or useless. How you react in these moments will define your ability to hit your goals. Someone who is incapable of reaching them will simply give in and allow the past to imprint itself onto their self-image and thus cause themselves damage.

What you must do is question the past and its emotions. This is not easy to do, but injecting a dose of rationality into proceedings always helps. When in the throes of emotion, ask yourself if your reaction is rational or not. Rationality does not mean you become a Vulcan and start viewing emotions as weak.

However, you need to understand that the past is simply a set of events. The person who carried out those actions doesn't exist anymore and, therefore, letting yourself be25 affected by those events is akin to you deeply reacting to someone else's experience.

This line of thought will not readily present itself in the moment, and it will be tough. But you must try. In other words, do something. You won't see progress for a while, but then one day, you'll find yourself automatically doing this when you feel low or when you feel things are closing in on you.

Like everything else, questioning the hold the past has over you is a habit and is in fact one of the success habits you must install within yourself. Stop letting the past hold you and step forward into your present. Fully utilize the power of your conscious mind to question and let go of it.

Awareness and the discipline to always do something when the past rears its head is the key for you to execute this challenge. Adversity is always going to hit you on your path. Just make sure you're not the one who is causing it and making things harder for yourself than they should be.

Welcome Adversity

Adversity, whenever it does occur, is often a sign that you're doing something correctly. Even if the current problems you're facing are the result of you screwing up something badly, the fact that adversity is here is a sign that you have a chance to make amends. This sort of thinking didn't come naturally to me, and there was a time when I regarded adversity as my cue to check out of the goal achieving process.

When you embark on a journey to achieve something, you will encounter failure. Previously, when I used to hit the first speed bump, I would immediately use this as an excuse to stop pursuing my goal. My reasoning was born out of a faulty understanding of what success looks like and what it is.

I bought into the faulty thought process that is often displayed in movies and pop culture with regard to achieving success. In these forms of media, you will often see that the only people who are successful are those who are impossibly intelligent and razor sharp, along with being impossibly good looking. They have abilities they were born with, and it stands to reason that they should be successful.

These people don't really need to work hard and even if they do, they do it in short bursts and inspiration strikes them easily. They easily achieve their goals, often right within the half hour or hour's time slot the show has. All of this led me to unconsciously mirror these beliefs in my life. And this is where the problem begins.

Life is not clean and does not resolve itself into easily understood plot threads. Adversity and problems always occur, and it especially presents itself to those who are successful. The fact is that the person who is more successful than the rest has simply overcome and faced greater degrees of challenges in their lives. None of this is good TV, so we don't see it on there.

Ask yourself if you're making the same mistake that I used to make. Are you believing the lie that is spread in pop culture about talent and success? Do you think success is something that comes about without hard work? Or do you believe that hard work is the result of not being successful enough at something?

You might not realize that you're holding such beliefs consciously so take the time to really dig deep within yourself to see if such thoughts exist. If you find that they do, start installing correct behaviors and beliefs immediately. Look around you and you'll find examples of people who are less talented than their peers but at the top of their field.

You'll find that the people who are on top are there because they worked hard and believed in their goals. Not because they were talented. Bill Gates had a knack for computer programming and loved doing it. However, it was his ability to work through the night for long stretches, sleeping for just two hours right on his keyboard, that created the first version of BASIC and launched Microsoft.

Steve Jobs built Apple into what it is today thanks to his fanatical adherence to his vision and goals. It is debatable whether he could write a single line of code, and yet he built one of the largest technology companies in the world. Where does talent fit into his success story?

Adversity and Fear

Such poorly conceived beliefs often scare us into giving up on our goals. Fear is one of the leading causes of failure. The crazy thing about fear is that it comes in various forms. There's the fear of failure, fear of success, fear of missing out, fear of heights, and on and on it goes. You know what F.E.A.R really is? It's False Evidence Appearing Real.

Every time fear raises its head it's a signal to you that growth lies in that direction. Fear is a very common thing to experience, and you should not be ashamed or deny its existence. However, you should have the courage to act despite it. Examining why fear arises is instructive, and you will understand why the acronym for fear is true.

As I mentioned earlier, your brain has two sections, broadly speaking, within it. There's the less evolved bird brain that is automatic and has limited reasoning capability, and there is the more evolved brain that is slower to respond and has the power to reason its way through challenges.

The bird brain is tasked with running programs that threaten your survival. This is a good thing because if you're faced with a mortal threat, the last thing you want to do is to stand there and reason your way out of it. You have a better chance of survival if you just run. This is what enabled your ancestors to survive when humans still lived in caves and forests.

As the more evolved brain began creating the world we live in today, something funny happened. We managed to eliminate the threats to our survival to the extent that other humans are our biggest threat. I mean, when was the last time you locked horns with a lion or a tiger?

Our modern lives have a ton of convenience, and this makes our bird brain remarkably unsuited for it.

Being an automatic mechanism, the bird brain has no way to determine or reason what a real threat is. It operates on sensory information alone. Thus, when it detects any sort of a challenge to your comfort zone or anything that is perceived by you as being a threat, it kicks in and overrides the more reasoned portion of your brain.

This leads to you succumbing to anxiety and experiencing the fight or flight response, where you feel on edge and can feel your heart beating at elevated levels, ready to help you run from some imaginary predator. When your bird brain continues to react like this over and over, it builds a neural network inside your head to where even the slightest threat justifies such an extreme response—and this is how anxiety and fear build up.

Notice throughout this entire process, there isn't a single threat to you physically. There is nothing that will cause you to die abruptly and nothing that presents a problem that you cannot work your way out of. Your mind uses fear to prevent you from working further because it thinks that fear is a sign of a mortal threat. After all, this is the dominant network within your head and this is how it's been behaving all this time.

Your fear itself is born out of false evidence. You're misinterpreting and believing the wrong things about events happening in your life and this is causing you to hurt yourself in the long run. Examine the reasons you've previously given up on your projects and goals, and you'll find that you've been listening to false evidence all along.

So if you know what F.E.A.R stands for, what does S.U.C.C.E.S.S stand for?

The Elements of Success

The nature of success is described for us by Dr. Maltz in his book *Psycho Cybernetics*. Briefly it stands for:

- S- Sense of direction
- U- Understanding
- C- Courage
- C- Compassion
- E- Esteem
- S- Self-acceptance
- S- Self-confidence

Let's look at these in more detail. The first S, which stands for sense of direction, is nothing but your goals. This is easily understood. Without knowing where you're going, how will you know you've arrived? Your goals are what everything else in your life flows from and the more aligned your daily life is with your goals, the more successful you will be.

Understanding refers to your ability to recognize what is needed to succeed and which beliefs help you the most. It refers to you not paying heed to harmful beliefs and stopping them in their tracks. Things such as acceptance of adversity and the ability to be solution-focused rather than problem-oriented are signs of someone who understands what it takes to achieve success, whether they've achieved it as of yet or not.

Courage is the ability to act in the face of fear. It is the easiest thing in the world to join the herd and behave like a sheep. We saw in a previous chapter how the herd mentality is one of the most powerful psychological effects that govern our decisions. Every time we go against the herd, the world seeks to impose fear upon us and tries to get us to conform. Having the courage of your convictions and the ability to act in the face of fear (by recognizing its true nature) is required in order to achieve your goals.

Compassion seems incongruent here, but it is a vital aspect of success. Everyone is on their own path, and this path is what they need in order to bring the best out of themselves. A lot of people succumb to the trap of starting to think that everyone else needs to live a certain way or that their way is the right way. This is true of people who are successful and those who are not. Compassion forces you to recognize your place in the world and that everyone has their own problems to deal with. It forces you to look outside of yourself and assess situations better.

Esteem refers to the level of respect you have for yourself. This and the next element, self-confidence, are really all about your self-image and what you believe about yourself to be true. I think you'd agree that it is pretty difficult to become successful without having confidence in your abilities and respecting your abilities to dig yourself out of a hole.

When all these various elements align themselves within you, you'll realize that you're well on your way to achieving everything you desire. At that point, adversity is not going to bother you since you'll recognize its true nature. After all, without adversity, how would you ever grow?

Increasing Resilience

There is no shortcut to increasing your resilience. Simply put, the more adversity you overcome, the more resilient you will be. How do you overcome that first bout of adversity, though? Well, the secret to overcoming fear and adversity is to reframe the problem.

You must have definitely heard of the glass half full versus glass half empty observation? How about the silver lining in the cloud? What are these but methods of reframing the problem and asking different questions?

I've already hinted at the method of reframing in the previous section. If you look at adversity as an opportunity to grow stronger, you'll actually look forward to it and welcome it! As you grow stronger, this is exactly what will happen. The thing you want to experience the most, as mentioned earlier, are higher levels of problems. You want those big, juicy ones to present themselves in your life so that you can overcome them and grow stronger.

This doesn't mean that you run around deliberately causing problems for yourself. Obviously, that is just being stupid. Life will throw enough problems your way to keep you busy, so don't worry about having no problems to deal with! Throughout the tough times, always remember that they don't last. Instead, it is tough people that do. Every overnight success story has been twenty years in the making.

There are some easy to implement strategies and tips you can use to build your resilience. Let's take a look at some of them now.

Connect

You don't have to go at it alone. Lean on someone you love and trust and confide in them. You're doing them a disservice by not sharing your burdens with them. It isn't just family you can lean on, join organizations or mastermind groups as well. One of the best ways of reducing the adversity in your life is to volunteer for a charity.

Working with charities helps to increase the degree of compassion in your life and you will view situations and people who have it far worse than you. Do you know that altruism is what makes us the happiest? Yup, we are happiest when we're helping others and giving stuff away for free.

This is why compassion and nurturing your ability to look beyond yourself is so valuable for your success. It is not a coincidence that the billionaires amongst us also happen to be the ones who give back more to society, as a group, than anyone else. So go ahead and assist someone who really needs help. Get outside your own head.

Stop Identifying

When a problem occurs, acknowledge that it has happened and move onto finding solutions for it. Unfortunately, what most people do is start building this problem into an insurmountable obstacle. They start identifying with the problem and begin to think it says something about them as individuals.

Statements such as "I'm such a loser" or "I'm failing at my goals" indicate someone who is identifying with the problem. The correct way to handle failure is to instead detach from it and stop making it about yourself. After all, the world does not revolve around you!

Frame your words about the incident in as objective a manner as possible. Instead of thinking "I failed" think "(the outcome) didn't happen." Stop placing yourself at the center of everything and you'll see that you gain a new perspective on your issues. What's more, it becomes easier to adopt a solution-oriented mindset, which is what will solve your problems for you.

Another excellent tactic is to adopt the view of someone you admire and has already achieved the goals you want to hit. If your goal is to become a world-class tennis player, think of how Roger Federer would handle this problem. Would he moan and complain about life not being fair? Or would he put his head down and get on with it?

What if Federer were here right now and saw you building mountains out of molehills? Would he respect you as his equal? Think along these lines and you'll bring yourself back to reality and face your problems with greater ease.

Discover Yourself

Every obstacle is an opportunity to find something out about yourself. So go ahead and discover yourself!

Look at problems as a method of really getting to know the real you and use them as tools of self-discovery.

Obstacles give you a chance to not only find yourself but to also strengthen your existing relationships and work processes. They give you the chance of becoming more robust and durable. So embrace them and find yourself.

Keep Moving

I mean this both literally and figuratively. When faced with a lot of worry and doubt, move your body. Exercise or even walking has great benefits in terms of reducing the stress within you. Maintain a healthy regimen of exercise in your life and strive to be as physically fit as you can and you'll find that you achieve greater levels of mental clarity.

Figuratively speaking, keep doing something that moves you closer to your goals. Some days you might take huge steps and some days minuscule ones. It doesn't matter. Keep doing something and keep showing up. Often, the days you feel terrible and don't feel like working turn out to be the best days for you to work deeply.

Keep showing up and hit your goals. It doesn't matter if they're big or small, just keep doing something. You'll continue chipping away at your problems, and one day, you'll find yourself dealing with a bigger, more challenging one. This is exactly what you want!

Avoid Detachment

This tip is more of a warning than anything else. When seeking to stop identifying with the problem, some people detach themselves from it completely and go to the other extreme of thinking it is happening to someone else. Ignoring your problem is not going to make it go away.

The cause of such a reaction is fear and if you observe this sort of behavior in yourself then take a long, hard look at how you deal with fear and what your beliefs are about it. Perhaps there's some harmful belief with regards to your self-image that is causing this behavior so examine that as well.

Be Kind to Yourself

This should be the first step, but I'm going to put it here to really get the point across to you. *Always* be kind to yourself! Treat yourself with respect and always remember that you deserve all the good things you want in life. You are fallible and make mistakes. This is perfectly fine.

The people who have achieved the goals you desire are exactly the same as you. They have self-doubts and suffer from anxious moments as well. Model their behavior and recognize that you, by yourself, are more than enough. Stay positive in your thinking and know that their same success can be yours.

So remember to take good care of yourself and always be aware of what is going on inside of your head. Success might be a long road and there will be obstacles along the way. Go easy on yourself and avoid harsh judgment. Hold yourself accountable, but don't admonish yourself just for the sake of it.

Above all else, remember that obstacles and adversity help you grow. So welcome them with open arms!

Conclusion

I still remember driving home from work that miserable day, having witnessed people enjoying luxuries that I couldn't afford. I was hurt. How could life be this cruel to me and why was it being this way? You could say I was being pretty emotional. After all, life had not turned out the way I wanted but, surely, I wasn't so unworthy so as to have simple pleasures denied to me?

As I said before, this worst moment of my life was actually the biggest blessing I have ever received. It enabled me to grow and achieve all the things I have in my life thus far. I have gone from a place of wondering why life was incredibly harsh to me to living the life greater than what I have ever dreamed of. There truly is nothing I cannot accomplish (physical limitations aside).

I have the firm belief that once I set my mind on a goal, I will achieve it. After all, I've done it multiple times in my life and as we all know, competence builds confidence. I know exactly where you are and I also know what sort of obstacles you are going to face. Well, maybe not exactly, but I certainly know their nature and how you will feel about them.

Understand this: your problems will get bigger, but you will find the process easier. This is because you will grow into a person you cannot even fathom right now.

Looking back, if you had told me during my lowest moment who I am today, I'd have been more inclined to believe that I could become a Martian!

Your brain cannot imagine the riches and prosperity in store for you. All you need to do is follow the steps outlined in this book. Granted, this is easier said than done, but nothing worth achieving is ever easy. It all starts with you sitting down with the willingness and desire to change your life and to recognize the massive power your goals have when it comes to building it.

Spend a lot of time thinking about and designing your BHAG and work backward from it to develop your SMART goals. Remember to think really big, and be prepared to take massive action to achieve your goals. Massive action involves deeply-focused work produced in large quantities, and it is tough to work in this fashion because you are simply not used to working this way.

Let go of the need to compare yourself to your peers or anyone else. You're unique. How can something unique be compared? Let go of the binds that social media and other forms of so-called connectivity impose upon you and instead embrace deep focus. Map out every moment of your day and always show up, no matter how terrible you feel.

You don't need to do everything every single day. Instead, do something every day. Keep moving forward and develop strategies to view obstacles for what they really are. Remember that success is not about being the most talented or the strongest. It is about being the most persistent and hardworking.

Adopt the view that when someone decides to do the same thing as you, only two outcomes exist. Either you work harder than them or you die. That's it. This is the same attitude that Will Smith adopts and if it works for him, it will work for you as well. Don't let anyone ever tell you that you don't deserve something or that you're not worthy of success. This is a lie.

The fact that it is a lie is easily demonstrated by observing the way you have been engineered by creation. You have the most powerful creative mechanism available at your disposal. Clear the cobwebs that currently surround it and put it to use. You will make mistakes along the way and that's fine. Mistakes by themselves are not the problem.

It is viewing them as the end of the world and refusing to learn from them that will cause your failure more than anything else. Remember how the learning process works. In order to learn something, you need to learn how not to do something, so mistakes really do help you learn. Embrace them and much like adversity, look forward to their occurrence so you afford yourself the opportunity to learn.

One of my greatest passions in life is to share the things I have learned so that people might benefit from them as I have. Knowledge only grows when it is shared, and let me tell you, I am a living testament to the fact that you do not need special talent or ability to hit your goals and achieve success in life.

You just need the right mentality and execution. So, having said all of that, I speak abundance and prosperity into your life! Embrace the new growth and development that lies ahead. The person you become while reaching your goals greatly exceeds what you get. Go ahead and make your mistakes! Go ahead and be who you are meant to be!

References

Boomer, J. 2014. "Whether You Think You Can, or Think You Can't ... You're Right." CPA Practice Advisor. https://www.cpapracticeadvisor.com/firm-management/article/11575149/whether-you-think-you-can-or-think-you-cant-youre-right (Accessed September 4, 2019).

Collins, J., and Porras, J. 2009. *Built to last.* New York, NY: Collins.

Harris, J. 2018. "The brain as a neural network: This is why we can't get along." Medium. https://towardsdatascience.com/the-brain-as-a-neural-network-this-is-why-we-cant-get-along-bd94bc7e49cc?gi=c8f15222d921 (accessed September 4, 2019).

Hendry, E. 2013. "7 Epic Fails Brought to You By the Genius Mind of Thomas Edison." Smithsonian. https://www.smithsonianmag.com/innovation/7-epic-fails-brought-to-you-by-the-genius-mind-of-thomas-edison-180947786/ (accessed September 4, 2019).

Hosie, R. 2017. "Is it impossible to change your personality past the age of 30?" The Independent. https://www.independent.co.uk/life-style/personality-change-past-age-30-is-it-possible-psychology-kirsten-godfrey-david-buss-carol-rothwell-a7757866.html (accessed September 4, 2019).

Koebler, J. 2019. "Elon Musk and Larry Page Have the World's Weirdest Friendship." Vice. https://www.vice.com/en_us/article/bmj4zz/elon-musk-and-larry-page-have-the-worlds-weirdest-friendship (accessed September 4, 2019).

Maltz, M. 1974. *Psycho-cybernetics*. New York: Pocket Books.

Mischel, W. 2014. *The marshmallow test*. New York: Little, Brown and Company.

Murphy, F. 2017. "The human brain isn't built on a file system." LinkedIn. https://www.linkedin.com/pulse/human-brain-isnt-built-file-system-frank-murphy (accessed September 4, 2019).

Newport, C. 2016. *Deep work*. New York, N.Y.: Grand Central Publishing.

Oshin, M. 2019. "Inversion: The Billionaire Thinking Skill You Were Never Taught in School." Mayo Oshin. https://mayooshin.com/inversion-charlie-munger-billionaire-thinking/ (accessed September 4, 2019).

Farnam Street. 2019. "The Buffett Formula: Going to Bed Smarter Than When You Woke Up." https://fs.blog/2013/05/the-buffett-formula/ (accessed September 4, 2019).

Whelan, C. 2018. "Lactic Acidosis: Symptoms, Causes, Treatment, and More." Healthline. https://www.healthline.com/health/lactic-acidosis (accessed September 4, 2019).

Wilczek, F. 2015. "Einstein's Parable of Quantum Insanity | Quanta Magazine." Quanta Magazine. https://www.quantamagazine.org/einsteins-parable-of-quantum-insanity-20150910/ (accessed September 4, 2019).

www.ingramcontent.com/pod-product-compliance
Lightning Source LLC
Chambersburg PA
CBHW070648220526
45466CB00001B/348